A Wildfire Risk Assessment Framework for Land and Resource Management

Joe H. Scott
Matthew P. Thompson
David E. Calkin

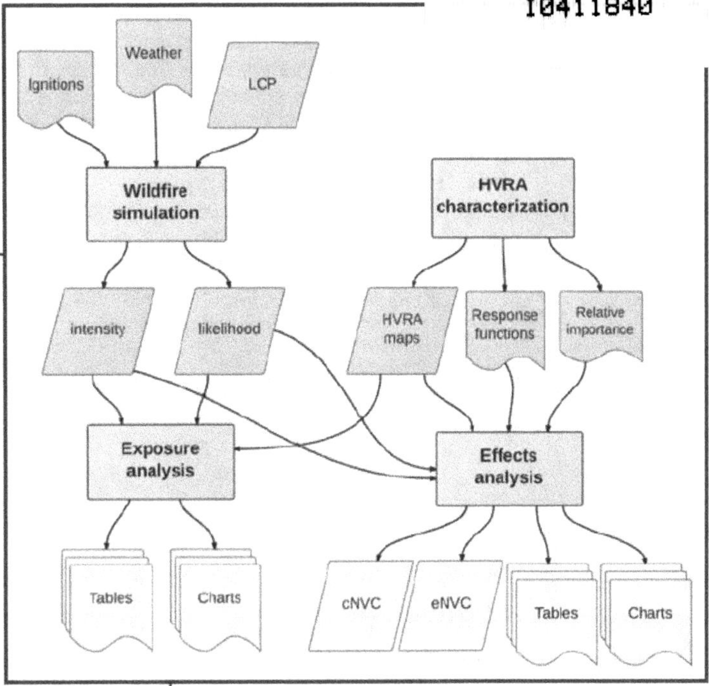

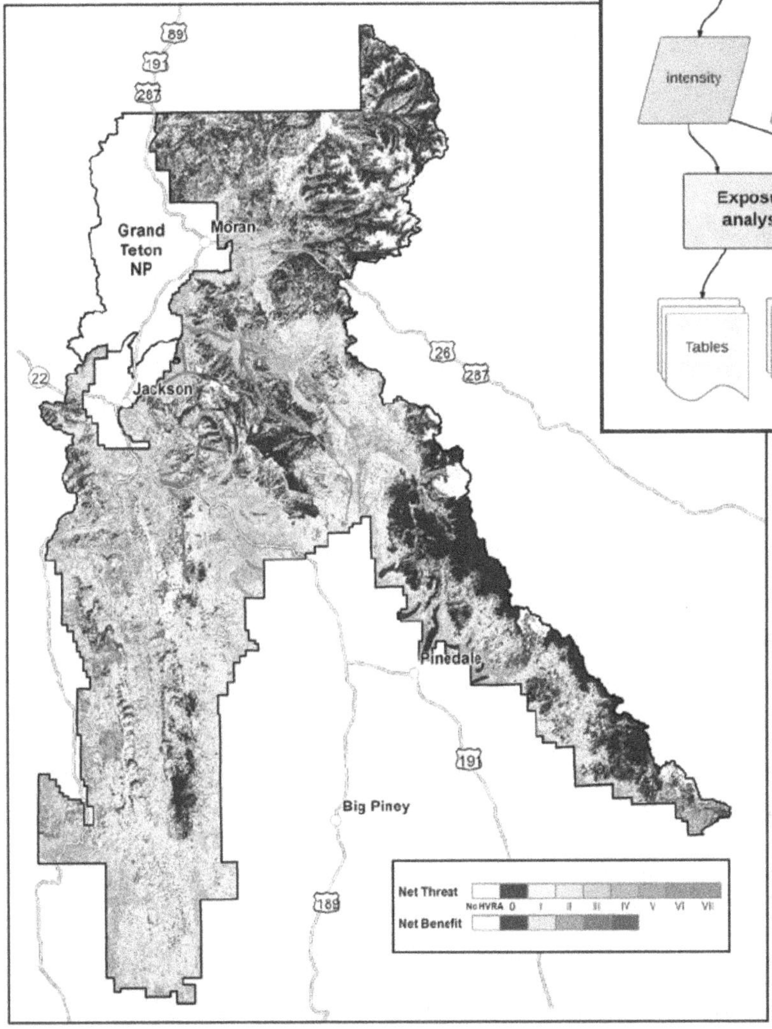

I0411840

United States Department of Agriculture / Forest Service
Rocky Mountain Research Station
General Technical Report RMRS-GTR-315
October 2013

Scott, Joe H.; Thompson, Matthew P.; Calkin, David E. 2013. **A wildfire risk assessment framework for land and resource management**. Gen. Tech. Rep. RMRS-GTR-315. U.S. Department of Agriculture, Forest Service, Rocky Mountain Research Station. 83 p.

Abstract

Wildfires can result in significant, long-lasting impacts to ecological, social, and economic systems. It is necessary, therefore, to identify and understand the risks posed by wildland fire, and to develop cost-effective mitigation strategies accordingly. This report presents a general framework with which to assess wildfire risk and explore mitigation options, and illustrates a process for implementing the framework. Two key strengths of the framework are its flexibility—allowing for a multitude of data sources, modeling techniques, and approaches to measuring risk—and its scalability, with potential application for project, forest, regional, and national planning. The specific risk assessment process we introduce is premised on three modeling approaches to characterize wildfire likelihood and intensity, fire effects, and the relative importance of highly valued resources and assets that could be impacted by wildfire. The spatial scope of the process is landscape-scale, and the temporal scope is short-term (that is, the temporal dynamics of succession and disturbance are not simulated). We highlight key information needs, provide guidance for use of fire simulation models and risk geo-processing tools, and demonstrate recent applications of the framework across planning scales. The aim of this report is to provide fire and land managers with a helpful set of guiding principles and tools for assessing and mitigating wildfire risk.

Keywords: hazard, exposure analysis, burn probability, fire intensity, effects analysis, landscape scale, geospatial

Authors

Joe H. Scott, Pyrologix LLC, Missoula, Montana

Matthew P. Thompson, USDA Forest Service, Rocky Mountain Research Station, Missoula, Montana

David E. Calkin, USDA Forest Service, Rocky Mountain Research Station, Missoula, Montana

You may order additional copies of this publication by sending your mailing information in label form through one of the following media. Please specify the publication title and number.

Publishing Services

Telephone	(970) 498-1392
FAX	(970) 498-1122
E-mail	rschneider@fs.fed.us
Web site	http://www.fs.fed.us/rmrs
Mailing Address	Publications Distribution Rocky Mountain Research Station 240 West Prospect Road Fort Collins, CO 80526

Foreword _____

This report envisions increasing adoption of risk assessment in wildfire management and planning, and seeks to facilitate this process by comprehensively describing a wildfire risk assessment framework as well as a toolkit for implementing the framework. Similarly, this report is premised on increasing sophistication within the fire modeling community, and the use of fire modeling outputs by managers to help support land and resource decisions. Embracing risk management principles is consistent with Federal wildfire policy as well as other significant efforts such as the National Cohesive Wildland Fire Management Strategy and the Collaborative Forest Landscape Restoration Program.

The recent emergence of risk-based decision support tools, in particular the Wildland Fire Decision Support System, suggest a trend towards reliance on quantitative, geospatial information regarding the likely occurrence, spread, and consequences of wildfire. The use of burn probability modeling techniques is a key component that can capture spatial variation in wildfire likelihood and intensity as a function of ignitions patterns, fire weather, topography, and fuel conditions. In turn, this information can help managers assess the likely exposure of highly valued resources and assets to wildfire, as well as the likely effects of being exposed to wildfire.

To be clear, risk assessments are not in and of themselves decision making tools, but rather provide information that can be useful in a broader decision making process. Assessment results can be applied across the wildfire management spectrum, depending upon the spatial and temporal scope of analysis. That is, managers may be interested in assessing the risks associated with an upcoming fire season, with a given escaped large wildfire, or with post-fire consequences and burned area emergency response. The framework and toolkit described in this report are most relevant to pre-fire planning, and can help inform decisions relating to ignition prevention, fuels management, and response planning. Applying the assessment framework can provide managers with a "snapshot" of current landscape conditions and associated risks. Periodic assessment over time can provide critical information for monitoring trends in risk and evaluating the performance of previous risk mitigation investments.

Who Can Benefit from Reading This Report?

We hope that fire managers, geospatial fire analysts, and resource specialists will all find value in this report. Managers and decision makers will be most interested in the overview of the assessment framework (sections 1 and 2), as well as the concluding sections describing the value of risk assessment and its role for informing decisions (sections 7 and 8). Fire analysts and resource specialists will also benefit from reading those sections; in addition, they will find details on how they may be called upon to help implement the framework and support decision processes.

i

Table of Contents

A Wildfire Risk Assessment Framework for Land and Resource Management

Joe H. Scott
Matthew P. Thompson
David E. Calkin

Unless there is an understanding of the type, likelihood, and magnitude of ecological changes that result from fire (either catastrophic fires or the controlled burns used as forest management tools), or conversely from the lack of fire, it will not be possible to quantify the relative risks and benefits associated with various fire management alternatives.

Fairbrother and Turnley (2005, p. 32)

1. Introduction

Wildfires—unplanned wildland fires—can result in significant, long-lasting impacts to ecological, social, and economic systems; therefore, it is necessary to identify and quantify the risks posed by wildfire, and to subsequently develop cost-effective mitigation strategies. To do so, fire and fuel managers require information on where fires are likely to occur, the intensity at which they might occur, and with what impacts to highly valued resources and assets (HVRAs; that is, the things we care about). Managers need to assess wildfire risk.

Risk assessment is a mature scientific approach to quantifying risk, and serves as a decision support tool that can inform strategic, operational, and tactical decision making. Analyzing risks helps managers make decisions where outcomes are inherently uncertain (Morgan and Henrion 1990). Recent developments in technology and decision support systems have improved the ability to assess, monitor, and respond to wildfire risk. Many in the fire management community are likely familiar with the Wildland Fire Decision Support System (WFDSS), which is premised on risk management principles (Noonan-Wright and others 2011). In the absence of wildfire risk assessments, decisions and management are likely to be less effective (Bar Massada and others 2009). Assessments of current conditions help land and resource managers (1) better understand how risks are distributed across their landscapes, (2) identify which HVRAs face the greatest expected loss (or benefit), and (3) inform decisions relating to preparedness planning and fuel treatment design. Further, evaluating how wildfire risk to HVRAs may change in response to alternative management scenarios through comparative risk assessment is a crucial component of risk-informed decision making (Calkin and others 2011a).

Fundamentally, wildfire risk analysis is about seeking answers to several important questions:

- How large are fires likely to grow?
- Which HVRAs have the greatest exposure to wildfire hazard?
- What are the likely effects to HVRAs of fire at different intensity levels?
- Where might fires cause harm/damage, and where might they lead to benefits?
- How is wildfire risk distributed across the landscape?
- Which areas are most likely to experience loss, how much loss, and to what HVRAs?

USDA Forest Service Gen. Tech. Rep. RMRS-GTR-315. 2013

1

Quantifying wildfire risk facilitates analysis of tradeoffs across HVRAs, and enables cost-effectiveness analysis as a basis for evaluating risk mitigation options (Thompson and Calkin 2011). A critical aspect of risk assessment is the use of probabilistic information to capture uncertainty surrounding the occurrence or intensity of hazardous events. Although we do not know with certainty where or when wildfires will occur, we can assemble information from climate and weather patterns, historical fire occurrence, fuel conditions, etc., to make an informed estimate of the likelihood of a given area experiencing a wildfire, or experiencing a wildfire of a given intensity.

The fundamental components for quantifying wildfire risk—likelihood, intensity, and susceptibility to effects (Scott 2006; Thompson and Calkin 2011; Miller and Ager 2012)—can be visualized as a Wildfire Risk Triangle (Figure 1). In this conceptual framework, fire intensity is a predictor of fire effects. Depending upon the HVRA and fire intensity level in question, fire effects could be negative or positive. Fire intensity is a robust fire characteristic that integrates two important fire characteristics—fuel consumption and spread rate. Other fire characteristics could be used in place of or in addition to fire intensity, but in this report we focus on the relationship between fire intensity and effects. Assessing wildfire risk requires quantifying potential wildfire intensity, quantifying its likelihood, and estimating the exposure and susceptibility of HVRAs to wildfire. These fundamental building blocks can be quantified and modeled in a variety of ways, and, in that sense, the risk assessment framework is quite flexible. The methods we promote and illustrate here are consistent with the scientific foundation for the Cohesive Strategy (Calkin and others 2011a), and have been increasingly applied for fire and land management planning applications at a variety of scales (Thompson and others 2011, 2013a).

The risk assessment framework is implemented in a geospatial context (Figure 2) that explicitly considers the location of HVRAs with respect to the three components of the wildfire risk triangle. The spatial interaction of wildfire likelihood and intensity with HVRAs is a key driver of wildfire risk (also known as exposure analysis). Further, the susceptibility or response of an HVRA to wildfire (termed "response function" in the figure) characterizes the likely fire-related losses and benefits to each HVRA included in the assessment.

Figure 1—The three building blocks of assessing wildfire risk are likelihood, intensity, and effects (Miller and Ager 2012; Thompson and Calkin 2011; Scott 2006). Implicit in this triangle is the assessment of risk to a particular HVRA, or a suite of HVRAs, and their spatial intersection with wildfire likelihood and intensity.

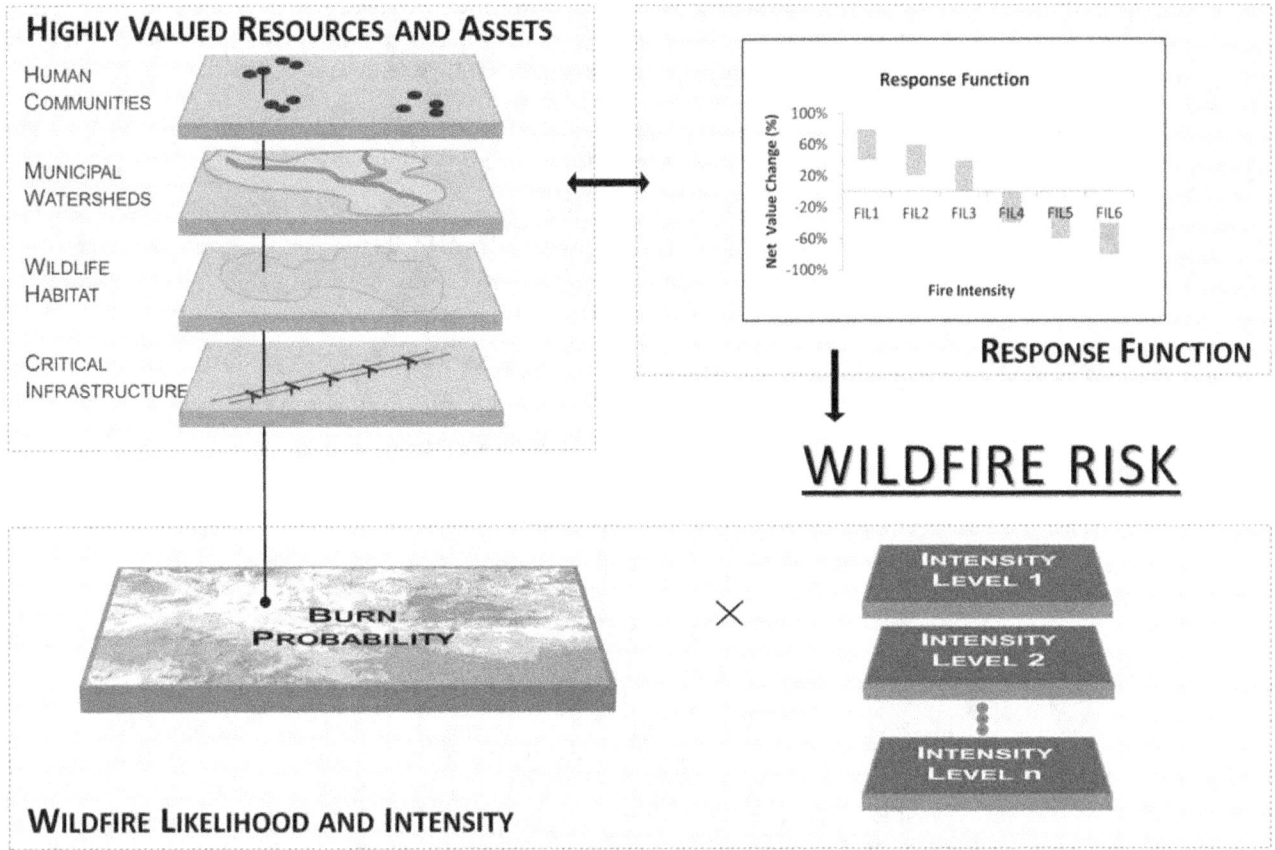

Figure 2—Geospatial context of wildfire risk assessment framework, explicitly recognizing the three components of the "risk triangle" in relation to the locations of HVRAs across the assessment landscape.

Risk assessments in and of themselves do not necessarily reveal appropriate mitigation strategies. Other factors to consider are relevant laws and regulations, strategic objectives, broader land and resource management plans (LRMPs), treatment opportunities, and likely effectiveness and negative consequences of various treatment alternatives. However, assessments of wildfire risk are critical for informing the development and implementation of cost effective risk mitigation efforts, and comparative risk assessment can be used as a basis to evaluate different treatment alternatives. That is, quantitative wildfire risk assessment serves as the yardstick by which to measure the effectiveness of mitigation alternatives. Designing efficient fire management strategies involves asking:

- Where can wildfire risk be best mitigated?
- What treatments and management activities are feasible?
- Where can different treatments be implemented, and to what extent?
- How will treatments affect various risk factors (likelihood and intensity)?
- How will treatments affect potential impacts to HVRAs?
- What combinations of activities can most cost-effectively mitigate wildfire risk?

The aim of this report is to provide fire and land managers with a helpful set of guiding principles and tools for assessing and mitigating wildfire risk. Key objectives of this report include ensuring that readers can:

- Understand basic concepts of wildfire hazard, exposure, and effects, and their relation to fire management;
- Define basic wildfire risk terms and concepts, and understand the major components of quantitative wildfire risk assessment;
- Interpret fire modeling outputs, principally burn probabilities and fireline intensities;
- Provide support to a wildfire risk assessment on their landscapes of interest; and
- Identify how to use wildfire hazard, exposure, and risk information in fire management plans and in fuel management prioritization.

Wildfire Hazard and Risk: Special Considerations

Wildfire can be Beneficial

When we think of the terms *hazard* and *risk* we generally think of the potential for loss. That is true for wildfire hazard and risk, but, in contrast with most hazardous natural phenomena, wildfires can also lead to substantial ecological benefits. Thus, in this report the notions of *hazard* and *risk* are expanded to recognize the potential for fire-related benefits as well as losses. As a result, the effects of wildfire are not quantified in terms of loss, but rather *net value change (NVC)*, considering the relative benefits and losses across fire intensity levels (Finney 2005). Unless otherwise noted, losses are identified as negative value change, and benefits as positive value change.

Wildfire is Spatial

Wildfire hazard is driven by complex interactions between ignitions, fuel, topography, and weather. Spatial variability in socioeconomic and biophysical characteristics influences spatial patterns in the frequency of natural and human-caused ignitions. Spatial variability in fuel conditions and terrain influences fire intensity and rate of spread. Fire spread direction (heading, flanking, backing, and points in between) also significantly influences fire intensity, and is itself influenced by fire spread characteristics of the broader landscape. Incorporating fire spread potential into the hazard assessment is especially important for large regions of the western United States where area burned is largely driven by spread from remote ignitions.

Wildfire Risk is Spatial

Wildfire risk is jointly determined by wildfire likelihood and intensity, HVRA exposure to wildfire, and the effects of wildfire on HVRAs. As described above, wildfire likelihood and intensity are both inherently spatial. Additionally, spatial variability in the location of HVRAs results in spatial heterogeneity in HVRA exposure to wildfire. And further, spatial variability in environmental characteristics can influence the magnitude and extent of potential for fire-related losses and benefits. Thus, all components of wildfire risk are inherently spatial.

Wildfire Management is Spatial

Spatial variability in expected losses and benefits can influence spatial variability in fire management objectives and priorities. This spatial information on wildfire risk can inform development of fire management plans and responses to wildfire. It can also inform design of fuel treatment, ignition prevention, or other risk mitigation strategies.

4

USDA Forest Service Gen. Tech. Rep. RMRS-GTR-315. 2013

In the subsequent sections we present a framework that quantifies wildfire risk, in a spatial context, that accommodates multiple HVRAs simultaneously. We then describe a proven process for implementing this framework, including a description of the primary modeling and analytical components, to help resource managers apply these concepts and tools to manage fire on their landscapes. Following this introduction we delve into the details of the risk modeling process, with specific guidance and instruction provided for fire and fuel modelers, decision analysts, resource specialists, and others supporting the risk assessment process. We then describe how information on wildfire hazard and risk can be incorporated into risk mitigation strategies, including pre-fire planning, fuel treatment design, and incident response. Multiple illustrations and real-world applications are highlighted, along with recommendations for future opportunities. Lastly, we conclude by describing the pros and cons of adopting and implementing the wildfire risk assessment framework.

2. Assessing Risk: From Concept to Analytical Approach

Concepts of Hazard and Risk

It is important to begin with a common understanding of terms and concepts used in wildfire hazard and risk assessment. The terms hazard and risk are related, but not synonymous. Hazard is a physical situation with the potential to cause damage to HVRAs (Scott 2007), resulting in loss (of value). In the wildfire context, the concept of wildfire hazard must be expanded to include the potential for beneficial changes to the HVRA that partially or wholly offset any damage. Characterization of hazard typically relates to physical properties of the natural phenomenon itself, for instance the height of sea-level rise associated with a coastal storm surge, or the speed of sustained wind in a tropical cyclone. In the wildfire context, we use measures of fire intensity—fireline intensity and flame length—as measures of wildfire hazard, although other measures such as fuel consumption or other fire characteristics may also be useful.

Assessment of wildfire risk further incorporates the likelihood that an HVRA will experience an event and the HVRA's susceptibility if it does (that is, consequences to the HVRAs resulting from exposure to varying intensity levels). The susceptibility of a home to coastal storm surge depends on construction materials and design. Thus, the amount of damage will vary for homes of different materials and design, even for the same storm surge height. Similarly, wildfire risk to HVRAs will vary with fire intensity level, their occurrence probabilities, and HVRA susceptibility. Thus, "risk" is conceptualized jointly as the likelihood, intensity, and susceptibility to effects of wildfires on HVRAs (see Figure 1). Fire intensity is the primary wildfire characteristic related to potential fire effects—typically, the greater the intensity the greater the loss, but this is not always the case.

Estimating risk entails estimating the exposure of HVRAs to a hazardous phenomenon, and the effects on the HVRA from that exposure (Thompson and Calkin 2011). Exposure analysis explores the potential spatial interactions of HVRAs with risk factors—fire likelihood and fire intensity—without considering how these factors affect HVRA value. In contrast, effects analysis explores the response of HVRAs to varying levels of these risk factors. Fire effects are often expressed as a percentage loss of value for a given intensity level. The effects of fire are driven by internal factors related to the HVRA itself as well as external factors related to the broader environment. For instance, post-fire impacts to water quality may be dictated not only by the intensity of fire but also the vegetation type and factors influencing erosive potential (soil type, slope steepness, precipitation patterns, etc.).

Expected net value change is a risk-neutral measure of the wildfire risk to resources and assets, and forms the basis for the quantitative wildfire risk assessment process. Equation 1 shows how the probability of fire burning in different fire intensity levels (BP_i, where i refers to the fire intensity class) and fire effects for those same classes, expressed as net value change (NVC_i) are combined to arrive at a quantification of risk in terms of expected net value change E(NVC). For a given HVRA, the equation sums losses and benefits (expressed together as NVC) for all n fire intensity levels multiplied by the probability of the area burning at a given intensity level (Finney 2005). Wildfire may present risk to any number of HVRAs that may be present at one location. In a later section we modify this equation to incorporate multiple HVRAs and to account for differences in relative importance across HVRAs. Although it is recognized that the flow of benefits and losses from a given fire may change over time, for the purposes of calculating risk with this equation a fixed period of time should be used.

$$E(NVC) = \sum_{i=1}^{n}(BP_i * NVC_i) \qquad [1]$$

There are four interrelated components to a comprehensive wildfire hazard and risk assessment (Figure 3). The wildfire simulation component uses tabular and geospatial input data regarding fuel, topography, weather and ignitions to produce geospatial outputs regarding burn probability and fire intensity. The HVRA characterization component identifies the resources and assets to include in the assessment, their locations on the landscape, their susceptibility to wildfire, and their relative importance. The exposure analysis component combines the fire simulation results with data regarding HVRA locations to produce tabular and graphical results depicting the wildfire simulation results where the HVRAs occur. Finally, the effects analysis component is similar to exposure analysis but also integrates the importance and susceptibility of HVRAs. Effects analysis is the implementation of equation 1, and produces the most comprehensive characterization of the potential for wildfire to cause a change in value, positive or negative, to an HVRA. The ability to characterize risk with a common measure E(NVC) facilitates integration of risk across multiple HVRAs, and allows for cost-effectiveness analysis as a basis for evaluating potential risk mitigation options.

Wildfire Likelihood and Intensity

Wildfire hazard is a physical situation with potential for wildfire to cause beneficial or negative impacts to HVRAs. The hazard that wildfire presents can be characterized rather simplistically as the occurrence of wildfire itself, but a more useful characterization also quantifies the potential intensity (or probability distribution of intensity) of a wildfire if it does occur. Within the wildfire risk framework it is further necessary to quantify the likelihood of a wildfire occurring (in some fields, this is called the hazard occurrence probability), be it the overall wildfire likelihood or the likelihood of wildfire occurring at a given fire intensity level.

Strictly speaking, fire intensity level is independent of likelihood (Miller and Ager 2012); they are separate measures. For our purposes, we will describe wildfire hazard in terms of both likelihood and intensity. This choice is driven by three key considerations. First, modern wildfire simulation models co-estimate likelihood and intensity, which are driven by a similar set of environmental factors. Second, as will be described below, a useful way to characterize hazard in a given location is often according to a probability distribution over wildfire intensity levels (Ager and others 2012; Scott and

6

USDA Forest Service Gen. Tech. Rep. RMRS-GTR-315. 2013

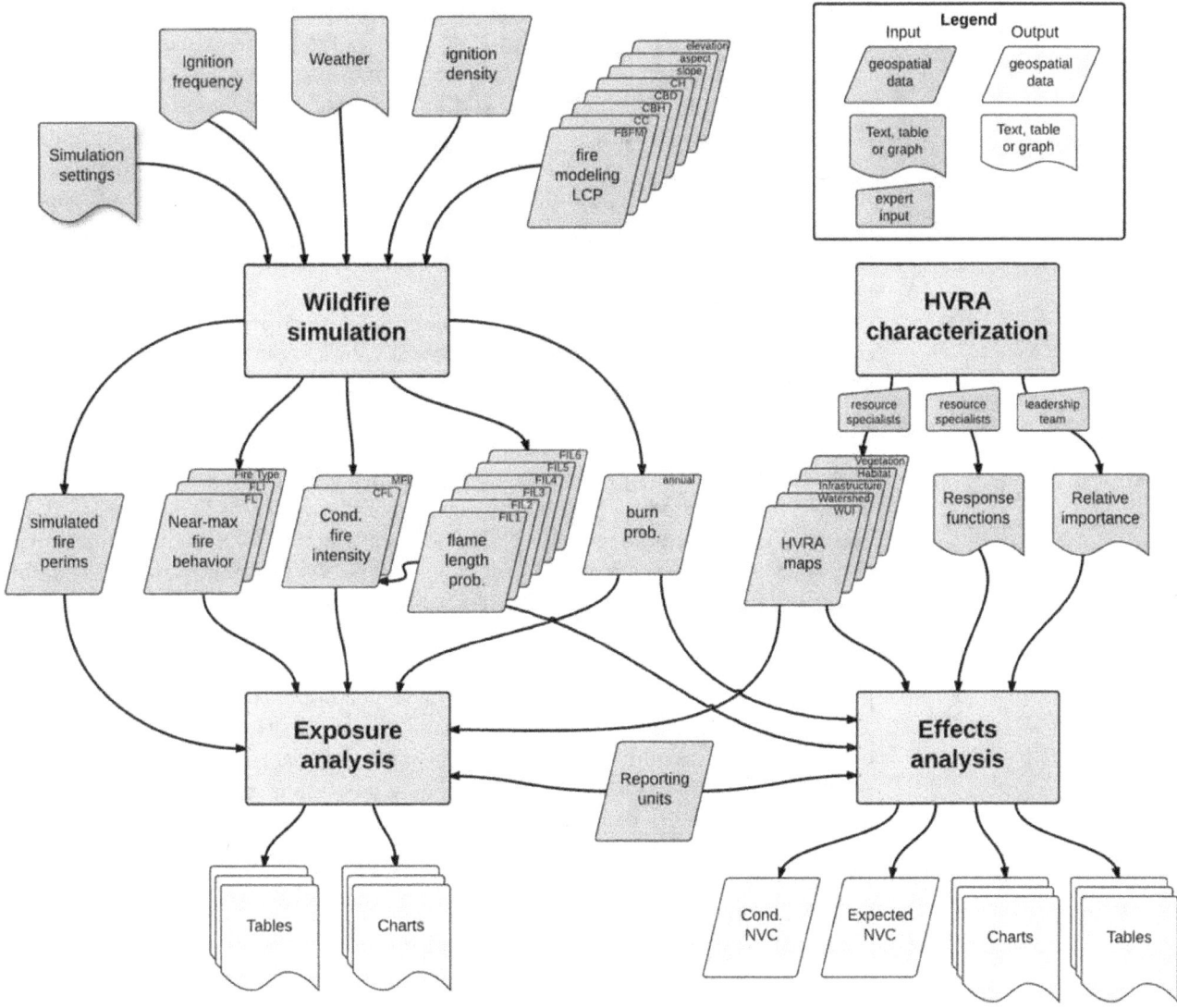

Figure 3—Process flowchart illustrating the relationships among the four components of the risk assessment process.

others 2012b). Further, and more intuitively, considering both likelihood and intensity as integrated measures of hazard fits with the concept of hazard as a situation with potential for damage. Consider two locations capable of producing identical wildfire intensities, but with different probabilities: one location is much more likely to experience wildfire than the other (due to higher ignition likelihood, for example). The location with higher likelihood to experience that wildfire intensity has a greater potential to cause damage, and therefore could be considered to be more hazardous. Taken together, wildfire likelihood and intensity are excellent quantitative measures of wildfire hazard.

The factors affecting wildfire intensity include the elements of the fire behavior triangle—fuel, weather, and topography—as well as spread direction (heading, flanking, backing, etc.). At a basic level, wildfire intensity can be assessed for a point, stand, or landscape without consideration of fire spread by assuming that a fire occurs at the given

USDA Forest Service Gen. Tech. Rep. RMRS-GTR-315. 2013

7

location(s) under specific weather, fuel moisture, and fire spread parameters (heading, flanking, or backing). Typically this is assessed as the near-maximum potential (for example, heading fire under 97th percentile fuel moisture and wind conditions). There may be a very low probability of a wildfire occurring under these conditions in any particular area, but nevertheless this level of assessment provides useful information about the potential wildfire behavior that different areas of a landscape are capable of producing. At the landscape scale, this type of wildfire hazard assessment may also be used to identify where on a landscape there is the potential to meet or exceed specific wildfire behavior thresholds, thus aiding the identification and prioritization of management opportunities.

In a complete assessment of wildfire hazard, wildfire occurrence and spread are simulated in order to characterize how temporal variability in weather and spatial variability in fuel, topography and ignition density influence wildfire likelihood across a landscape. In such cases, the hazard assessment includes modeling of burn probability, which quantifies the likelihood that a wildfire will burn a given point—typically a single grid cell (pixel)—during a specified period of time. Burn probability assessments can quantify the likelihood of wildfire of any intensity occurring or the likelihood of wildfire occurring at different fire intensity classes. Burn probability for fire management planning applications is often reported on an annual basis—the probability of burning during a single fire season. A distinguishing factor of modeling annual burn probability is the additional simulation of ignition probability and fire duration, in order to account for the relative frequencies and spatial patterns of historical ignitions. Alternatively, some planning applications report the burn probability *conditional* on a fire occurring during a specified "problem fire" weather scenario. Wildfire incident management applications, by contrast, express burn probabilities for a single fire over a matter of days or weeks.

Although some approaches to characterizing wildfire hazard do not include likelihood, burn probability modeling plays a major role in characterizing the potential for wildfire to cause effects, especially where analysts are interested in modeling fire spread with variable combinations of ignition location and weather conditions. Some wildfire modeling systems output fire behavior metrics in terms of probabilities, and therefore quantification of wildfire hazard will essentially have a probabilistic component. Typical outputs of probabilistic hazard assessment include summaries and maps of overall burn probability, burn probability by fire intensity level, mean wildfire intensity or flame length (that is, averaged over all simulations, incorporating non-heading spread direction and a range of simulated weather conditions), and the expected value of wildfire intensity/flame length calculated as the sum-product of burn probability and mean wildfire intensity/flame length.

Exposure Analysis

After characterizing wildfire hazard, the next critical step in assessing wildfire risk is exposure analysis. Wildfire exposure analysis refers to assessing the wildfire intensity and burn probability in locations where HVRAs are present. Thus this analytical step is premised on the ability to consistently map all HVRAs over the entire spatial extent of analysis. Exposure can be quantified in many ways, including summary statistics such as expected area burned or mean burn probability or mean fire intensity across mapped HVRA pixels. Wildfire exposure assessment has broad applicability in forest planning. Readers may be familiar with Rapid Assessment of Values at Risk (RAVAR) maps (Calkin and others 2011b) that assess exposure from an ongoing wildfire incident. Exposure analysis can also be used in National Environmental Policy Act (NEPA) assessments to compare differences in exposure of HVRAs under multiple alternatives or in National Forest Management Act (NFMA) and Forest Plan revision projects to identify HVRAs that are most likely to interact with wildfire and where on the landscape those wildfires are most likely to occur. Other potential applications include revising fire management plans, and assessing the likelihood of remote ignitions impacting specific HVRAs under different fire management scenarios (Scott And Others 2012a).

Effects Analysis

The next step in the assessment process is to identify how HVRAs are affected by wildfire. Predicting and quantifying fire effects can be very complex and challenging, especially for many ecological and other non-market HVRAs (Venn and Calkin 2011). The impacts of fire vary across spatial and temporal scales, and future disturbances or other uncertain processes influence those impacts. Predicting fire effects is challenged by limited or inadequate empirical observations, a lack of predictive models, and gaps in core fire science and fire effects science (Hyde and others 2013). Nevertheless estimating HVRA response to wildfire is a crucial step for quantitative risk assessment and for prioritizing mitigation efforts (Fairbrother and Turnley 2005).

Analyzing the susceptibility of HVRAs to varying levels of fire intensity relies on a combination of fire effects modeling and expert judgment. Despite availability of models for first-order fire effects (for example, tree mortality, soil heating, fuel consumption, and smoke emissions), some level of inference is still necessary to characterize the second-order effects (for example, sedimentation, habitat loss) in which managers are typically more interested (Reinhardt and Dickinson 2010). In some cases fire effects models may exist for a particular HVRA, perhaps a habitat suitability model that can account for fire. In most circumstances proxies or reliance on expert judgment may be required.

Fire effects analysis captures both fire-related benefits and losses, and is quantified in terms of value change, expressed in relative terms on a percentage basis (for example, complete loss = –100 percent). In this framework, expert-defined "response functions" translate fire effects into value change, based upon fire intensity and potentially other environmental characteristics. These response functions output a common measure of wildfire risk across market and non-market HVRAs.

Relative Importance and Relative Extent

The risk framework accommodates a variety of HVRAs using a common measure (*NVC*); when integrating the risk of wildfire to multiple coincident HVRAs it is important to incorporate the relative importance (*RI*) of HVRAs. That is, a weighted summation of risk [E(*wNVC*)] across HVRAs might be more representative of the broader social consequences of losses and benefits, and should reflect fire management objectives and priorities. For instance, the same degree of E(*NVC*) may be weighed differently across human communities, municipal watersheds, recreational areas, and wildlife habitat. If we were able to readily make value comparisons across market and non-market HVRAs in terms of monetary value (for example, dollars) then the articulation of *RI* would be straightforward. However a number of challenges preclude the use of non-market valuation and the definition of response functions in terms of monetary value for most practical applications (Venn and Calkin 2011).

Fortunately, multi-criteria decision analysis techniques can be employed to help balance and quantify tradeoffs and to articulate preferences and *RI* of HVRAs (Kiker and others 2005; Ananda and Herath 2009).The establishment of *RI* weights across HVRAs enables the weighted integration of risk across multiple HVRAs, allows for simpler mapping and visualization, and can facilitate prioritization decisions. Equation 2 illustrates the calculation of E(*wNVC*), which extends Equation 1 to integrate any number (*j*) of HVRAs. That is, E(*wNVC*) is complementary to, and not a substitute for, the single-HVRA E(*NVC*) values. Thus, articulating *RI* scores serves only to further enrich the results of assessing risks.

$$E(wNVC) = \sum_j \sum_i \left(BP_i * NVC_{ij} * \frac{RI_j}{RE_j} \right) \qquad [2]$$

The relative importance of different HVRAs is partitioned spatially according to the HVRA's relative extent (*RE*). Relative extent can be measured in any unit of measure (for example, number of hectares or grid cells). An HVRA that is extensively mapped will receive a lower relative importance value per unit area, whereas an HVRA that is rare on the landscape will receive a higher relative importance value per unit area.

Primary Modeling Steps

In order to quantify and characterize risks across any landscape, it is critical to have input from local staff, in particular line officers and resource specialists. Figure 4 outlines the primary steps of our analysis process to estimate wildfire risk. Step 1 (wildfire simulation) entails obtaining and updating fuel data layers, analyzing historical fire weather and fire occurrence, and outputs spatially resolved estimates of fire likelihood and intensity. Step 2 entails the elicitation of expert judgment from resource specialists regarding which HVRAs to assess and how fire may affect them. Step 3 uses multi-criteria decision analysis to establish relative importance weights across HVRAs.

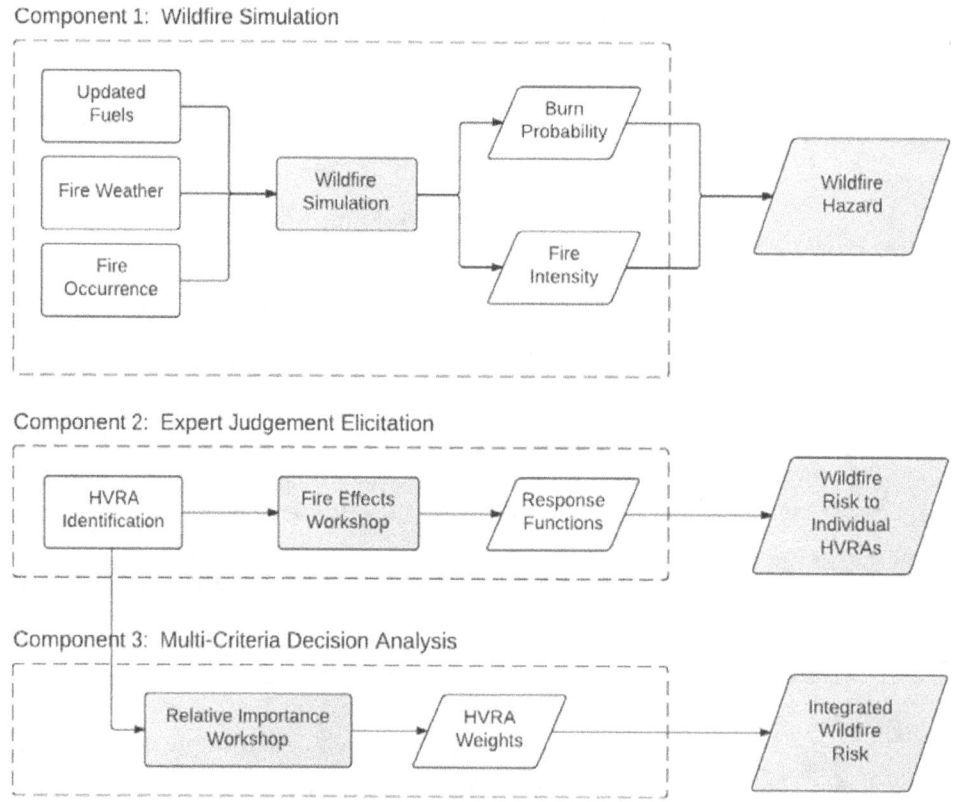

Figure 4—Conceptual flowchart for integrated wildfire risk assessment process, with three primary analytical components identified (Thompson and others 2013a).

Quantifying Wildfire Risk

Risk is a composite measure of expected consequences, calculated from the probability of a set of possible outcomes and their associated consequences. Wildfire risk is a composite measure of expected consequences of wildfire, calculated from the probability of fire occurring at various fire intensity levels and the losses and benefits to HVRAs associated with each fire intensity level. A comprehensive depiction of risk describes the full range of fire intensity probabilities and associated outcomes. Risk can also be expressed on a probabilistic basis for particular outcomes, for instance a 15 percent chance of fire-related losses exceeding a certain threshold. More common is to use a probabilistic expectation of net value change across all possible fire intensity levels (see Equation 1). An expectation is the sum-product of fire intensity burn probabilities and net value change. This approach does have potential pitfalls: variability around the expectation is not captured, and low-likelihood, high-magnitude events are equated with high-likelihood, low-magnitude events (Hanewinkel and others 2010). However, reducing risk to a single index nonetheless aids comparison of risk across complex landscapes where the sheer numbers to consider can be overwhelming.

Landscape-scale risk calculations will include the aggregation of risk to multiple HVRAs in multiple locations, and will incorporate relative importance and relative extent weights. Here we begin with a simple illustration of expected value. Consider a given landscape pixel housing an HVRA that we know will experience total loss if exposed to fire of any intensity. That is, the response of this HVRA to fire is –100 percent (see sections 4 and 6). If the probability of the pixel burning is 0.05, the expected net value change for that pixel is –100 * 0.05 = –5.00 percent. Now assume that fire effects do vary with fire intensity, with only –20 percent loss for low intensity fire (probability = 0.04), and –100 percent loss for high intensity fire (probability = 0.01). In this case the expected net value change for the pixel is –20 * 0.04 ±100 * 0.01 = –1.80 percent. Calculations proceed similarly across additional fire intensity levels and responses can be positive in addition to negative.

In an expanded example, consider two geographically distinct landscape pixels that each house two HVRAs: critical infrastructure, and fire-dependent habitat. The table below displays the response functions for each HVRA according to fire intensity level (flame length category). Whereas fire is universally bad for critical infrastructure, low to moderate intensity fire can incur a benefit for the fire-dependent habitat. In both cases, as intensity increases so does the potential for loss.

Fire Intensity Level	1	2	3	4	5	6
Flame Length Range (feet)	0 – 2	2 – 4	4 – 6	6 – 8	8 – 12	12+
Critical Infrastructure	–50	–60	–70	–80	–90	–100
Habitat	60	40	20	–20	–40	–

On the first landscape pixel (pixel A), there is an annual burn probability of 0.0155, and the distribution of burn probabilities by fire intensity level is shifted towards lower intensities (the fire intensity probabilities sum to 0.0155). The second landscape pixel (pixel B) has the same annual burn probability of 0.0155, but the distribution across fire intensity levels is shifted towards higher fire intensity levels.

(Continued on next page)

USDA Forest Service Gen. Tech. Rep. RMRS-GTR-315. 2013

11

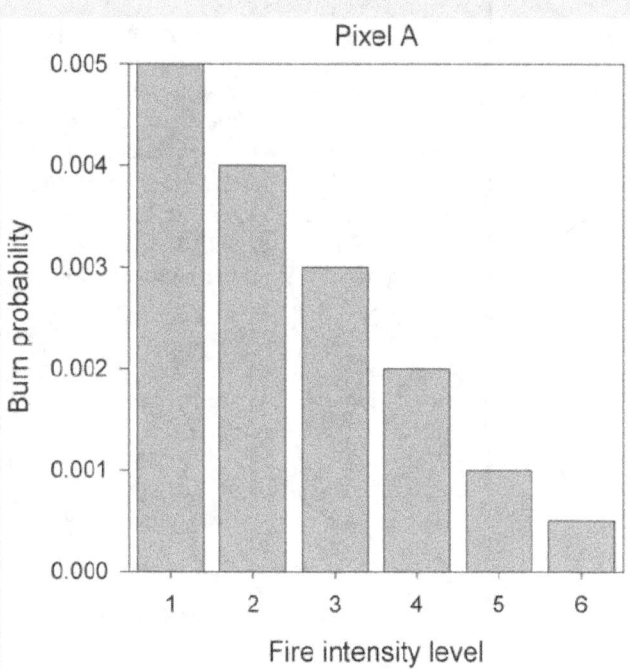

The expected net value change for critical infrastructure can be calculated as: $(-50 * 0.005) + (-60 * 0.004) + (-70 * 0.003) + (-80 * 0.002) + (-90 * 0.001) + (-100 * 0.0005) = -1.00$. For the fire-dependent habitat, by contrast, the expected net value change is positive at 0.41. This result is due to the combined effects of beneficial effects of low intensity fire and a greater likelihood of the area burning with low intensity.

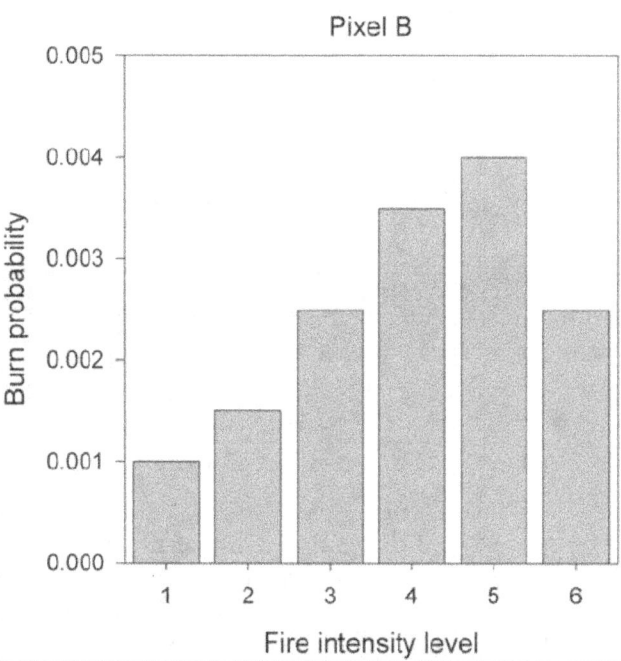

On landscape B the expected net value change is −1.21 for critical infrastructure, and −0.21 for the fire-dependent habitat. Because of the higher likelihood of higher intensity fire, a net loss is anticipated for the fire-dependent habitat. Thus wildfire hazard and HVRA response to fire jointly affect the spatial distribution of risk across landscapes.

Preparing to Implement the Framework

Broadly speaking, risk assessment is about more than the mere quantification of risk. The assessment process is comprised of three primary steps: problem formulation, problem analysis, and risk characterization. Problem formulation is a crucial first step; each analysis must be crafted to the specific management context and to address specific management objectives. Formulating the problem includes defining the spatial and temporal scope of analysis, the HVRAs to be included, the assessment objectives, and the intended use of the assessment results. The goal of the analysis phase is to estimate the likelihood of HVRA exposure to varying levels of wildfire intensity, and to predict HVRA responses resulting from exposure to varying levels of wildfire intensity. Lastly, risk characterization summarizes risks posed to various HVRAs, interprets the risk estimates, and evaluates uncertainties. Figure 5 summarizes this entire process.

The first stage in a risk assessment is to clearly formulate the problem to be solved, which in many cases may relate to a statement of purpose and need. Another important step is to identify the spatial and temporal scale of analysis. For the framework presented here, the spatial scale of analysis is landscape (in other words, not stand based or tree based), with the ultimate scope dictated by the size of the landscape under consideration. The framework itself is theoretically amenable to landscapes of any size, contingent upon availability and sufficiency of geospatial data and processing capacity. Geographically, the process we emphasize in this report is more amenable to areas where fire spread is

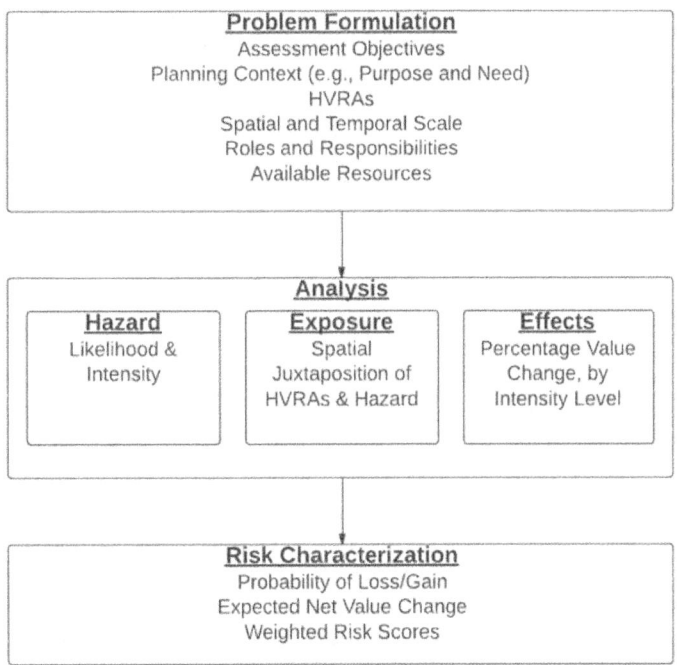

Figure 5—The primary steps of the wildfire risk assessment. First the problem is formulated, including definition of the assessment objectives, the planning context, the HVRAs to be included, and the spatial and temporal scope of analysis. The primary analytical components identify and quantify hazards, HVRA exposure, and fire effects. Lastly, risk characterization summarizes risks posed to various HVRAs.

the predominant source of fire occurrence and "large" fires account for the majority of acres burned. The temporal scale for the process is over the short-term, including only the more immediate post-fire impacts; the wildfire modeling approach generates burn probabilities given current conditions, without modeling the long-term dynamics of post-fire recovery, succession, or disturbance. As projections go further into the future, the degree of uncertainty associated with predicting fire effects will tend to increase.

Setting the stage for this type of risk assessment will not come without effort. The time spent upfront organizing and clarifying the assessment process is important, however, and should pay dividends in the long run through a more streamlined analysis process and, ideally, through improved decision making. Fire and land managers and decision makers looking to implement this process should start by considering (1) the state of geospatial data, (2) the time and resources available for the assessment, (3) the role for leadership, (4) the role for resource specialists and other staff, and (5) the number and extent of HVRAs to be considered.

State of Geospatial Data—Current and accurate data is necessary for essentially every component of modeling and evaluating wildfire risk. Compiling a usable, accurate, valid, and complete geospatial dataset is one of the biggest hurdles of the entire risk assessment process. Historical fire weather and fire occurrence data are required to parameterize fire models. Spatial information on vegetative conditions is necessary to define the "fuelscape" over which simulated fires will grow. The location of HVRAs with respect to wildfire hazard will determine their exposure, and other environmental characteristics could codetermine fire effects.

Time and Resources Available for the Assessment—Typically, implementing the risk assessment framework requires a series of workshops to calibrate fuels, critique fire modeling outputs, define response functions, and define relative importance weights. These workshops will involve different levels of commitment from different types of individuals. The workshops themselves can take place over the course of a few days, although a significantly greater level of commitment is necessary prior to the workshops. A primary resource-intensive component is the compilation and stewardship of geospatial data. Modeling wildfire occurrence and behavior is another intensive activity that may require additional support depending on local fire modeling expertise. Agency-provided support could stem from the Fire Modeling Institute (www.firelab.org/fmi), the National Fire Decision Support Center, or the Enterprise Program, although external options could also be appropriate.

Role for Leadership—In effect, the information used within a risk assessment and broader risk management process can be divided into two types: values-based and science-based. A clear delineation of these types of information helps provide transparency and rigor to the decision process (Gregory and Long 2009). It is the responsibility of leadership to provide values-based information in the form of management objectives and priorities and in the context of fire protection and restoration. This value-based information does not, of course, reflect the personal values of any individual line officer or resource manager, but rather reflects the values of society at large, as expressed through laws, regulations, agency mission, stakeholder participation, etc. This includes identifying the objectives of the assessment, identifying which HVRAs should be included in the assessment, and defining the relative importance weights, if desired, to differentiate risk scores across HVRAs.

Role for Resource Specialists and Other Staff—It is the role of specialists and staff to provide science-based information. This can come in many forms, for instance provision of geospatial data regarding fuels or HVRA locations. Principally, resource specialist expertise is sought for the purposes of defining HVRA-specific response functions. Ideally the disciplinary backgrounds represented are well aligned with the HVRAs being assessed, for example, wildlife biology for critical habitat; soil science and hydrology for watershed response, etc.

Number and Extent of HVRAs to be Considered—On any landscape there are likely to be multiple resources and assets that could be impacted by fire. These could include the wildland urban interface (WUI), critical infrastructure, municipal watersheds, sites of cultural or historical importance, habitat for a variety of aquatic and terrestrial species, recreational sites, experimental forests, timber resources, etc. For this type of mid-scale assessment, however, it is typically sufficient to identify a handful (3-8) of the most important (that is, the most highly valued) resources and assets. Which HVRAs are of the greatest concern, or figure prominently in land and fire management plans? This "big picture" perspective enables an understanding of major patterns and likely impacts of risk, and can set the stage for further more refined analysis if necessary.

Addressing Uncertainties

Estimating wildfire risk is no easy task, and requires confronting multiple sources of uncertainty. First, and perhaps most obviously, we cannot with perfect accuracy predict the location and timing of fire occurrence, nor can we predict the weather driving fire behavior after an ignition (variability as a source of uncertainty). Second, although we know that not all fire is universally bad or universally good, it is difficult to project the relative fire-related losses and/or benefits to many HVRAs (limited knowledge as a source of uncertainty). Further, comparing benefits and losses across at-risk HVRAs can seem like an apples and oranges comparison, so to speak, especially when considering non-market HVRAs and trying to balance societal values. It can be difficult to balance priorities across HVRAs and to establish relative importance weights (unknown or ill-formed preferences as a source of uncertainty).

The risk assessment process outlined in this report is specifically tailored to address each of these sources of uncertainty. Different decision support tools and approaches are more appropriate for different manifestations of uncertainty. Table 1 outlines how the specific modeling approaches in this framework—probabilistic wildfire modeling, expert-based fire effects modeling, and multi-criteria decision analysis—relate to key components of risk and corresponding uncertainties.

Table 1—Three key components of the wildfire risk assessment framework, their respective predominant uncertainty type, and the corresponding methodology to appropriately manage uncertainty (modified from Thompson and Calkin 2011).

Wildland fire context	Type of uncertainty	Methodology
Fire likelihood and intensity	Variability	Probabilistic modeling
Fire effects	Knowledge	Expert judgment
Relative importance of HVRAs	Preference	Multi-criteria decision analysis

USDA Forest Service Gen. Tech. Rep. RMRS-GTR-315. 2013

15

3. Wildfire Simulation

Wildfire hazard is a physical situation with potential for wildfire to cause harm to persons or damage to resources or assets. Wildfire intensity is the primary wildfire characteristic related to the potential for harm or damage—typically, the greater the intensity, the greater the potential for harm or damage. The primary factors affecting wildfire intensity—fuel, weather, and topography—therefore also affect wildfire hazard.

The likelihood of experiencing a wildfire is included in this section as a measure of wildfire hazard. Taken together, wildfire likelihood and intensity are excellent quantitative measures of wildfire hazard; both are also used in the quantitative risk assessment framework described in an earlier section. In this section we focus on analytical methods, modeling tools and model results useful for characterizing wildfire likelihood and behavior, primarily wildfire intensity. Although wildfire intensity for any discrete point on the landscape can be simulated independent of its surroundings, wildfire likelihood depends on geospatial context across a broad area. Therefore, we focus on geospatial assessment of wildfire hazard across a landscape rather than at a discrete point.

As mentioned above, the three main factors of the fire behavior triangle—fuel, weather, and topography—affect wildfire intensity. A fourth factor also strongly affects wildfire intensity: relative spread direction (heading, flanking, backing, and all points in between). For the same fire environment, wildfire intensity is greatest at the head and declines quickly along the flanks and rear where the flame front is oriented across or against the heading direction. Measures of conditional fire intensity described in this section incorporate the effect of spread direction, while near-maximum potential wildfire intensity does not—it is calculated in the heading direction only. Additionally, ignition frequency and density across a landscape influence wildfire likelihood.

Of the fire modeling systems capable of producing wildfire likelihood (Table 2), FSim—the large-fire simulator (Finney and others 2011b)—is particularly well-suited for a comprehensive hazard and risk assessment because it implicitly simulates all significant wildfires (the large ones that account for approximately 95 percent of the area burned), it incorporates the effects of fire suppression on wildfire containment, it addresses variability of fuel moisture, wind speed and wind direction as it historically varies throughout the fire season, and it simulates wildfire occurrence on an annualized basis.

Table 2—Review of the characteristics of three widely -used fire modeling systems that model natural variability with probabilities.

Characteristic	FSPro	FlamMap5	FSim
Planning context and decisions supported	Suppression strategy development	Fuel treatment planning, "problem fire" analysis	Fire management plan development, preparedness and response planning, fuel treatment planning
Duration	Days to weeks	One to a few burning periods	Entire fire season
Fires considered	Individual escaped fire	Problem fire ignitions	All large fire ignitions
Simulation type	One fire, many weather scenarios	Problem fires, extreme weather scenarios	All fires, all weather scenarios
Type of burn probability	Conditional on current fire location and specified time period	Conditional on specified weather scenario	Annual (full fire season)
Source of Variation	Wind speed, wind direction, fuel moisture content, fuelscape	Ignition locations, fuelscape	Wind speed, wind direction, fuel moisture content, fuelscape, ignition location, ignition probability, containment probability, fire duration

FlamMap5 (Finney 2006) produces outputs similar to FSim, but the results are 'conditional' in that they pertain to the condition that an escaped fire has occurred. The more limiting factor, however, is that FlamMap5 typically does not simulate the very largest fires that can occur on a landscape, and it is those very large fires that tend to contribute to wildfire likelihood. FlamMap5 is an excellent choice of modeling system if the resources available for the hazard and risk assessment preclude the use of FSim.

We mention FSPro (Finney and others 2011a)—for 'fire spread probability'—primarily for completeness. Many of the landscape-scale concepts we discuss in this report apply to the incident level as well. At the incident level, FSPro is the most appropriate modeling system for estimating wildfire likelihood over the expected life of the incident (days to weeks). FSPro does not currently produce conditional fire intensity outputs. If it were modified to do so, the same risk calculations described here could be applied to FSPro results to estimate incident-level hazard and risk, potentially providing even more detailed decision information than currently available.

Three broad classes of input data are required when using a fire behavior modeling system for geospatial assessment of wildfire hazard: a fire modeling landscape, historical weather data, and historical fire occurrence data (Figure 6). The wildfire simulation component produces three broad measures of wildfire hazard: the near-maximum potential wildfire behavior that hypothetically could occur, the likelihood that wildfire will reach a given location (burn probability), and the mean wildfire intensity given that it does burn (conditional fire intensity). The development of these simulation inputs and interpretation of the outputs are described in the following sections.

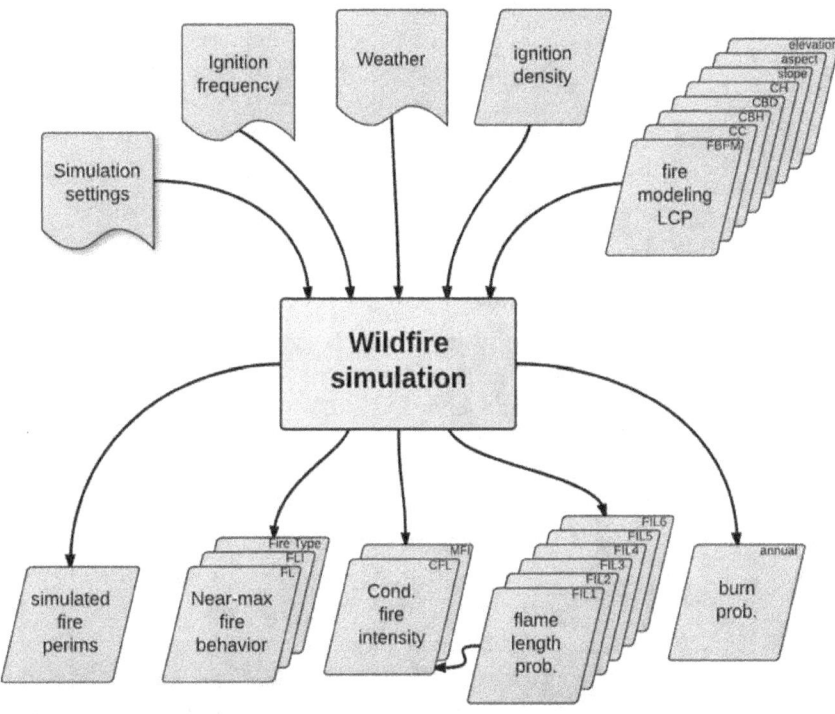

Figure 6—The wildfire simulation component of the overall wildfire risk assessment process uses tabular and geospatial data regarding fuel, weather, topography and ignitions to produce geospatial data regarding the near-maximum fire behavior, conditional fire intensity, flame-length probability and burn probability. These outputs are inputs to the exposure analysis and effects analysis components.

Fire Modeling Landscape

A fire modeling landscape is a raster-format geospatial characterization of the fuel, vegetation, and topography inputs needed for simulating the full range of wildfire behavior—from surface fire through active crown fire—based on separate models of surface fire spread (Rothermel 1972), crown fire spread (Rothermel 1991), and the transition between them (Van Wagner 1977). Those inputs include surface fuel characteristics (fire behavior fuel model), canopy fuel characteristics (canopy base height, canopy bulk density), forest vegetation (forest canopy cover and height), and topography (slope steepness, aspect, and elevation). Geospatial fire modeling systems require the fire modeling landscape data in the form of a fire modeling landscape file (LCP), the file format originally developed for FARSITE (Finney 1998) but now also used in FlamMap5 and FSim. The LCP file consists of several raster data layers—one for each characteristic. Each raster data layer is a grid of cells, or pixels, where each cell contains a numerical value that indicates something about the layer. For example, each cell in the fuel model layer contains a coded value indicating the fuel model assigned to that cell.

The fire modeling landscape must meet certain characteristics to be suitable for geospatial assessment of wildfire hazard. The fire modeling landscape must have complete, wall-to-wall coverage across all ownerships, especially if a fire growth modeling system is to be utilized, so that simulated fires can spread across all parts of the landscape. Not only must the data cover the entire landscape extent, but the methods used to produce them should be consistent. Many locally available datasets do not meet these criteria because they were developed for only a portion of the required landscape extent (clipped to an administrative boundary, for example). Mixing data sources in a single landscape is not recommended because doing so can potentially affect the results and conclusions of the assessment.

For an assessment that relies on fire growth simulation to estimate wildfire likelihood, the extent of the fire modeling landscape must be larger than the primary area of interest in order to account for the effect of distant fires reaching the area of interest. A buffer of 15-30 km (10-20 mi) is usually sufficient, but specific landscape conditions could require an even larger buffer. For example, large areas of grass or grass-shrub fuel in the buffer area could allow fires to spread more than 20 miles, especially if strong winds are possible.

The appropriate resolution (the dimensions of each grid cell or pixel) of the fire modeling landscape depends on the landscape extent and requirements of the fire modeling systems used. Generally, the larger the landscape extent, the larger the cell size will be. A landscape consisting of more than 50 million cells is unwieldy to use in any fire modeling system; 10 million cells is a reasonable upper limit on a fire modeling landscape. Note that even if the primary area of interest were a single point, the buffer area suggested above would encompass roughly 250,000 to 1 million acres. Most assessments will therefore require a cell size between 30 m and 270 m.

Much of the geospatial data for creating a fire modeling landscape is available at a 30-m cell size, and must therefore be re-sampled to the coarser resolutions using a geographic information system (GIS). Several resampling methods are available in a GIS; the "nearest-neighbor" method is recommended because it ensures that widely scattered or narrow, linear elements of the fuelscape—like riparian stringers or roadways—remain represented in the re-sampled layers in proportion to their initial representation. The "majority" resampling method tends to eliminate those features, homogenizing the landscape by making the most prevalent fuel types even more prevalent.

An important characteristic of geospatial data is its projection, which is a set of parameters required for characterizing geospatial information on the Earth's surface as a 2-dimensional map. The map projection of the fire modeling landscape data is critical for its subsequent use in any fire growth modeling system because those systems implicitly assume that grid north is true north. Some map projections are designed to minimize the distortion of area across a large landscape, but those map projections can result in true north being nearly 20 degrees different than grid north in some parts of the continental United States. A projected coordinate system specifies the map projection and other reference parameters needed to calculate geospatial relationships. For fire behavior modeling, the ideal (and most commonly used) projected coordinate system is Universal Transverse Mercator (UTM), which balances distortion in distance, direction, shape, and area within a UTM zone. The best-fit UTM zone is the zone that contains the center of the landscape.

Data Sources—A fire modeling landscape can be obtained from a variety of sources or generated using a variety of methods. The LANDFIRE project (www.landfire.gov) publishes all of the required fuel, vegetation and topography rasters, both as separate rasters and as a complete LCP file, at a 30-m cell size, for the continental United States, Alaska, and Hawaii. In addition to the required rasters, LANDFIRE also publishes the underlying vegetation rasters (existing vegetation type, cover, and height; biophysical setting), a disturbance raster (which indicates disturbance type, severity, and time since disturbance) and the fuel mapping rulesets used to generate the fuel and vegetation rasters of the LCP. These underlying rasters and rulesets can be used to critique, edit, and update the published rasters, resulting in a locally calibrated fire modeling landscape.

Locally produced vegetation data can sometimes be used to generate one or more rasters of the fire modeling landscape, but several challenges exist. First, such data are often not produced for all land ownerships within the landscape extent, so the requirement for completeness may not be met. Second, these data are often produced in polygon format, with relatively large land areas mapped to the same fuel or vegetation characteristic. While it is easy to convert the polygon data to the required raster format, the resulting layers frequently miss small areas of important fuel or vegetation conditions, especially when those conditions are barriers to fire spread like rock outcroppings or riparian areas, and tend to homogenize the fuelscape. Lastly, locally produced vegetation rasters often consist of only vegetation cover type and not the associated vegetation characteristics of vegetation cover and height, which are useful for distinguishing among fuel models and canopy characteristics.

Regardless of how the fire modeling landscape is acquired or generated, a thorough critique should be performed (Stratton 2006, 2009) to ensure that no errors in producing the landscape have occurred.

Tools—The computer tools required to acquire or develop a fire modeling landscape depend on the method. The required LCP characteristics described above suggest that LANDFIRE will be a major source of the required layers, so in this section we will focus on the tools needed to work with those layers. It is possible to download an LCP file directly from the LANDFIRE Data Distribution Site (http://landfire.cr.usgs.gov/viewer/) without using GIS software. This downloaded LCP file can be critiqued and edited (using relatively rudimentary editing tools) using a combination of geospatial fire modeling systems (FlamMap5 and FARSITE). Far more powerful editing and analysis tools are available using a GIS such as ESRI's ArcMap with the Spatial Analyst extension. A variety of custom toolbars have been developed specifically to work with fire modeling landscape and related rasters in ArcMap. The LANDFIRE Data Access Tool (LFDAT; www.niftt.gov) is an ArcMap Toolbar that works in conjunction with the LANDFIRE Data Distribution Site, allowing the user to specify the extent of the fire modeling landscape using existing geospatial datasets (such as a buffered boundary around the analysis area). LFDAT also includes several useful utilities, including one for creating an LCP file from the edited rasters and another for splitting an LCP into separate rasters.

LANDFIRE has made available the LANDFIRE Total Fuel Change (LFTFC; www.niftt.gov) Toolbar, a powerful tool for editing a fuelscape. To use the LFTFC Toolbar, the user downloads the underlying vegetation layers (biophysical setting; existing vegetation type cover and height) and disturbance layer (indicating disturbance type, severity, and elapsed time since disturbance). The fuel mapping rules for each LANDFIRE mapping zone are contained in a database within the LFTFC Toolbar; the user can import and edit the fuel mapping rules or update the disturbance raster to reflect disturbance since the last version of LANDFIRE data. From this information, the LFTFC Toolbar generates the fuel and vegetation layers required for the LCP.

Finally, the 'LCP critique' function of FlamMap5 (www.firemodels.org) provides a basic assessment of LCP characteristics and the layers it contains. In addition to landscape-wide summaries, 'LCP Critique' summarizes the landscape characteristics where each of the surface fuel models exists.

Historical Weather Analysis

The acquisition and analysis of historical weather data representative of the fire modeling landscape is the next step in a geospatial assessment of wildfire hazard. Datasets archived by the Desert Research Institute (www.raws.dri.edu) from Remote Automated Weather Stations (RAWS) are the principal source of historical weather data for a wildfire hazard assessment. On many landscapes, a single RAWS can be selected to represent the entire landscape, but large landscapes may need to be broken into weather zones with a different RAWS assigned to each zone. The selected RAWS should be representative of the larger landscape (or zone), not just the local area around the RAWS. For example, a station located in the bottom of a deep valley is not a good candidate if its location results in primarily up- and down-valley wind directions, or if temperature and precipitation conditions in the surrounding mountains differ significantly from the valley bottom. Instead, a RAWS located on an upper slope or ridge may better represent the conditions under which wildfires burn.

Two types of weather data are needed: *hourly* wind data (speed and direction) and *daily* fuel moisture content (MC) data. Hourly wind data are typically available for a shorter historical period of time than daily fuel moisture observations. Ideally, a complete, year-long record of daily observations should be available for the selected station for a period of 20-30 years. A longer record is not necessarily desirable if weather conditions beyond that time no longer represent current conditions. Also, for maximum utility, the time period of these daily observations must coincide with the time period for historical fire occurrence. The longest available period of hourly wind data at a station can be used, regardless of coincident fire occurrence data, because the wind data are used only to populate monthly wind speed and direction distributions and not to correlate with fire occurrence. Wind speed measurements at RAWS stations correspond to a height of 6 m (20 ft) above the ground (or vegetation, if present).

Archived weather data can be used to calculate several indices of fire danger. The Energy Release Component (ERC) of the National Fire Danger Rating System (NFDRS) is the fire danger index most commonly used in fire management planning.

20

USDA Forest Service Gen. Tech. Rep. RMRS-GTR-315. 2013

Adjustments—Hourly wind speed data consist of the mean speed during the 10-minute period at the end of the hour, called the 10-min average, and the maximum instantaneous wind speed occurring any time during the hour, called the gust speed. Analysis of wind speed data for use in fire modeling can use either the 10-minute average, the gust, or both types of wind speed measurement. However, it has been suggested that a third wind speed type—the 1-minute average wind speed—may be better suited to some fire modeling applications than those two recorded wind types (Stratton 2006). Crosby and Chandler (1966) provide a table of conversions between the 10-minute average and the probable maximum 1-minute average during those 10 minutes. Depending on the fire behavior modeling system being used, converting to the 1-minute average wind speed can either be done as a simple hand calculation or as an update query in the wind speed database.

Each weather station contains an indication of the fire danger rating fuel model assigned to the station. However, it has been found that fire danger rating fuel model G is well suited to the purpose of relating the effect of fuel moisture to fire occurrence (Andrews and others 2003), regardless of the fuel model assigned to the station, because fuel model G contains fuel load in all size classes, including 1000-h timelag fuel particles (Finney and others 2011b). Therefore, we suggest changing the fire danger rating fuel model to "G" in FireFamily Plus before continuing with the analysis. We refer to calculation of *ERC* for fuel model G as *ERC-G*.

Tools—The main software tool for analyzing weather data is FireFamily Plus 4.1 (www.firemodels.org), but additional custom charts or tables can be generated in a spreadsheet or graphing program.

Historical Fire Occurrence

The acquisition and analysis of historical wildfire occurrence data within the fire modeling landscape is the next step in preparing for a wildfire hazard assessment. The minimum fire occurrence dataset consists of just three variables for each wildfire igniting within the fire modeling landscape: start (or discovery) date, start location, and final fire size. Because "large" fires burn the majority of land area (Strauss and others 1989)—contributing most to wildfire hazard—the fire occurrence dataset needs to be accurate for large fires; the completeness and accuracy for small fires is much less important. There is no single definition of a large fire for use across the United States, but typically a size threshold of 100-300 acres is used. Small fires contained during initial attack are critically important for preparedness planning because they represent wildfires that did not burn much of the landscape. However, because those small fires do not contribute much to area burned, they are not important to consider when assessing wildfire likelihood assuming the historical level of preparedness and initial attack success continues.

Just like information about fuel characteristics, fire occurrence data must be complete for the entire landscape, regardless of jurisdictional boundaries. This requirement presents a challenge because fire occurrence data are compiled separately by each jurisdiction across a landscape, with little effort to coordinate. For example, the same wildfire event could be recorded in multiple fire occurrence databases if more than one jurisdiction responded to the event. The duplicates must be removed before continuing with the analysis. Wildfires originating on private land may not be recorded in any fire occurrence database, especially if they are contained during initial attack. Fortunately, the large fires we are most interested in tend to be well captured in the available databases.

Like weather data, fire occurrence data is desired for a period of 20-30 years. A shorter period of fire occurrence data may not capture the true nature of fire occurrence on the landscape, and a longer period may include the influence of a past climate that no longer reflects current conditions.

USDA Forest Service Gen. Tech. Rep. RMRS-GTR-315. 2013

21

Data Sources—Several sources of historical fire occurrence data are available. Local land management units (an individual national forest, for example) usually have excellent records for wildfires originating within their own jurisdictions. Fire occurrence data for a variety of jurisdictions are available from the National Fire and Aviation Management Web Applications website (https://fam.nwcg.gov/fam-web/). Such datasets may contain duplicate records if different agencies record the same wildfire in their respective datasets. This situation can occur when an agency responding to the incident records the wildfire even though it starts in another jurisdiction. Eliminating duplicate records is a challenging but necessary exercise when compiling datasets across jurisdictions. Ensuring that all wildfires occurring on the analysis landscape are recorded is another challenge, especially for wildfires occurring on land for which a Federal or state agency is not primarily responsible for suppression.

For use in its own analyses, the Fire Program Analysis (FPA) project has compiled and critiqued nationwide fire occurrence data (Short 2013). This dataset is an excellent starting point for the generation of historical fire occurrence data for a fire modeling landscape, especially if the primary interest is fires that escape initial attack and become "large."

Tools—Several software tools are necessary or useful for compiling and summarizing fire occurrence data, regardless of the source. First, because the fire occurrence dataset must be attributed to a known portion of the landscape, it will be necessary to work with the dataset in a GIS. At a minimum, GIS is used to select the records that apply to the fire modeling landscape or other designated fire occurrence area. GIS may also be used in conjunction with the location and characteristics of those records to produce a raster of spatial ignition likelihood (density). FireFamily Plus is a standard software system for processing and analyzing fire occurrence data alongside historical fire weather data. FireFamily Plus can be used to generate specific inputs to fire behavior modeling systems such as FlamMap5 and FSim. Finally, spreadsheet software can be used for custom analysis of fire occurrence data. Pivot tables are especially useful for summarizing historical fire occurrence by size, date, etc.

Near-Maximum Wildfire Behavior

It is often desirable to assess the near-maximum wildfire behavior possible at each pixel on a landscape. The near-maximum wildfire behavior is an assessment of headfire behavior for a severe weather condition (though usually not the most severe possible). Several measures of wildfire behavior can be assessed in addition to wildfire intensity, including the type of fire. With effort, it is also possible to quantify indices of crown fire potential. In this section we will focus on the most common measures: type of fire, fireline intensity, and flame length.

The first step in assessing near-maximum wildfire behavior is quantifying the severe weather condition in terms of wind speed, wind direction, fuel moisture, and spread direction. Near-maximum wildfire behavior is always calculated in the direction of maximum spread, representing a headfire. However, no standard exists for determining the weather condition to use, except that it is typically near, but not at, the most extreme values observed during the historical period. The (year-round) 97th percentile value of the probable maximum 1-minute average wind speed is a reasonable wind speed to use, applied in the upslope direction on all pixels regardless of aspect. Likewise, the 97th percentile dead fuel moisture contents are reasonable values to use for the near-maximum condition. Moisture content values for live herbaceous and live woody fuel particles must be determined from experience. A live herbaceous moisture content of 30-45 percent, representing fully to near-fully cured grass and herbaceous fuel, and a live woody moisture content of 60-90 percent, should work well for the near-maximum condition.

Type of Fire—The type of fire expected for the weather scenario is the most basic characterization of potential wildfire behavior. Geospatial fire modeling systems inherently classify type of fire into four classes: non-burnable, surface fire, passive crown fire, and active crown fire. However, that classification includes two very different fire types within the surface fire class—fires burning in a surface fuelbed with no canopy into which fire can move, and fires burning beneath a forest canopy because the transition criteria is not met. An updated classification may prove useful in distinguishing potential fire behavior (Table 3). A non-forest fire is defined as one for which there is no overlying forest canopy into which a fire could possibly transition. Here, we suggest a simple test for canopy cover to identify these situations. This type of fire will apply mainly to grasslands and shrublands, but areas temporarily deforested—such as young clearcuts or stands that recently experienced stand-replacing fire—will also be included. The surface fire type is then reserved for situations in which there is an overlying canopy in which a crown fire could develop, if conditions were amenable. Distinguishing non-forest from surface fire is a very straightforward calculation in ArcMap.

Fireline Intensity—Fireline intensity (*FLI*) is the rate of heat release per unit length of flaming fire front (kW/m), regardless of flame front depth (Byram 1959). Fireline intensity, also known as Byram's fire intensity or, in Canada, frontal fire intensity, is a fundamental fire characteristic containing "…about as much information about a fire's behavior as can be crammed into one number" (Van Wagner 1977). Fireline intensity is calculated from basic fire behavior and fuel particle characteristics:

$$FLI = H * W_f * \left(\frac{R}{60}\right) \qquad [3]$$

where H is the fuel particle low heat of combustion (kJ/kg), Wf is the load (mass per unit area) of fuel consumed in the flaming fire front (kg/m^2), and R is the linear rate of spread of the flame front (m/min) in the direction perpendicular to the fire front.

Rate of spread for use in Equation 3 is the linear rate of advance of the fire front in the direction normal to the fire front (see Catchpole and others 1982). Rate of spread on an actively spreading fire is estimated by observing the position of the fire front at different points in time. Rate of spread of surface fires (Rothermel 1972; Albini 1976) and crown fires (Rothermel 1991; Cruz and others 2005) can also be simulated using mathematical models. The overall spread rate of a wildfire, whether surface or crown, is simulated by combining separate surface and crown fire models into a coherent system (Finney 1998; Scott and Reinhardt 2001).

Table 3—An updated five-category type-of-fire classification. The original 'surface fire' category is divided into two classes: non-forest and surface fire. A non-forest fire is a fire burning where crown fire is not possible due to the absence of an overlying forest canopy. A surface fire is one for which an overlying forest canopy is present but the crown fire initiation criterion was not met.

FlamMap5 type of fire	Additional criteria	Five-category type of fire classification
Non-burnable		Non-burnable
Surface fire	CC[a] = 0	Non-forest
	CC > 0	Surface fire
Passive crown fire		Passive crown fire
Active crown fire		Active crown fire

[a]CC = canopy cover

Although more difficult to conceptualize than flame length, fireline intensity is a more scientifically robust measure of wildfire intensity, and does not require of the use of separate models for surface and crown fires. Classifying fireline intensity by its common logarithm has proven useful for mapping and summarizing fireline intensity results (Table 4). The relationship between fireline intensity and flame length is illustrated in Figure 7.

Table 4—Classification of fireline intensity based on the common logarithm of Byram's fireline intensity when measured in kW/m.

Fireline intensity range	(kW/m)	Fireline intensity class	
≥	<		
	3.162	I–	I
3.162	10	I+	I
10	31.62	II–	II
31.62	100	II+	II
100	316.2	III–	III
316.2	1,000	III+	III
1,000	3,162	IV–	IV
3,162	10,000	IV+	IV
10,000	31,620	V–	V
31,620		V+	V

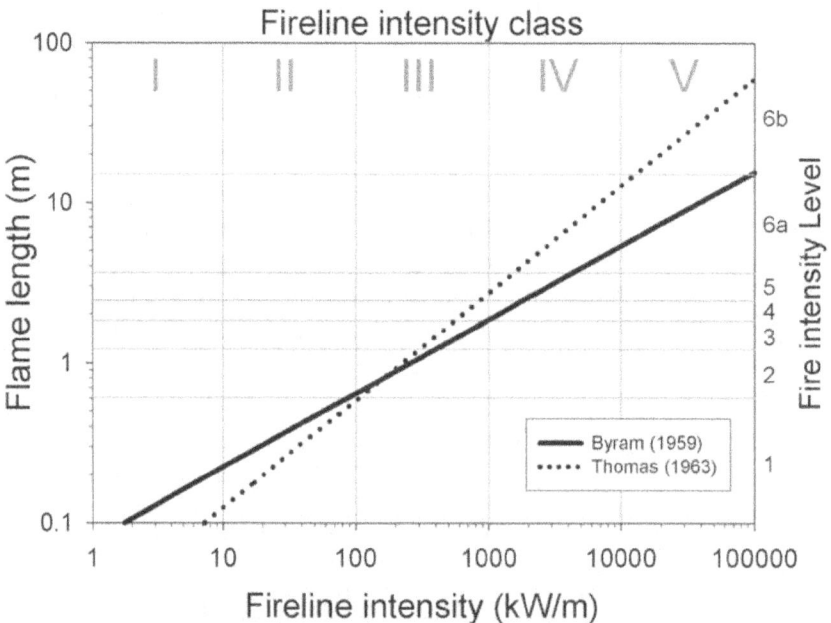

Figure 7—Illustration of a classification of fireline intensity based on its common logarithm. The chart also shows the difference between the Byram (1959) and Thomas (1963) relationships between fireline intensity and flame length. In geospatial modeling systems, the Byram model is applied to surface fires and the Thomas model is applied to passive and active crown fires. Note the common logarithm scaling of both axes. The six standard fire intensity levels (FILs) are indicated for reference. FIL6, corresponding to flame lengths greater than 12 feet, has been split at 50 feet.

Flame Length—Flame length is often the preferred measure of fire intensity for its easy conceptualization; it is estimated from the more scientifically robust fireline intensity measure described above. Two flame-length models are used, one for surface fires (Byram 1959) and another, predicting longer flames for a given fireline intensity, is used for passive and active crown fires (Thomas 1963). The difference is predicted flame length for a given fireline intensity as shown in Figure 7.

Like fireline intensity, flame length is a continuous variable that must be classified for mapping and other applications. The Fire Program Analysis program (FPA) classifies flame length into six standard fire intensity levels (FILs; Roose and others 2008). These FILs are reasonable classes for creating a map legend, but an additional class break at 15 m (50 ft) may be useful for distinguishing high intensity crown fires in conifer forests from intense surface fires in shrub fuels (Table 5).

Tools—FlamMap5 is the standard software system for generating near-maximum fire behavior characteristics across a fire modeling landscape. Nonetheless, a GIS is required to generate meaningful summaries of those results.

Wildfire Likelihood

Wildfire likelihood at a point on the landscape is measured as the annual or conditional burn probability (*BP*). Annual *BP* is the probability that a wildfire will burn a given pixel during a single calendar year. Conditional *BP* is the probability that a wildfire occurring during a specified weather condition will burn a given pixel, given that a fire does occur in that weather condition somewhere in the landscape. Conditional burn probabilities are relative, but not annual. Both annual and conditional *BP* are estimated across landscapes as the relative frequency of burning using a stochastic (or Monte Carlo) wildfire simulation system, which simulates thousands of iterations and then integrates those results. FSim produces annual *BP* results, while FlamMap5 produces conditional *BP* results. In both simulation systems, thousands to tens of thousands of iterations are simulated. An FSim iteration is the simulation of fire occurrence and growth on the landscape for a one-year period. A FlamMap5 iteration is the occurrence of a wildfire under a designated weather scenario. *BP* at a pixel is calculated as the number of iterations that resulted in that pixel burning divided by the total number of iterations.

Table 5—Flame length range associated with the six standard fire intensity levels (FILs) as defined by Roose and others (2008) and used in FSim. FIL6 is not split in FSim results; the split shown here is used to classify near-maximum flame length.

Fire intensity level	Flame-length range	
	- - m - -	- - ft - -
FIL1	0-0.6	0-2
FIL2	0.6-1.2	2-4
FIL3	1.2-1.8	4-6
FIL4	1.8-2.4	6-8
FIL5	2.4-3.7	8-12
FIL6a	3.7-15	12-50
FIL6b	15+	50+

Measures of Likelihood—Burn probability is most commonly expressed as a decimal fraction, theoretically varying from 0 to 1. Annual *BP* is generally quite a low value—very often less than 0.01—making its expression as a fraction difficult to visualize or interpret. An alternative is to express *BP* in terms of "odds" rather than a decimal fraction. The odds of a wildfire occurring is the ratio of the number of iterations that resulted in a pixel burning to the number that did not. For example, a *BP* of exactly 0.01 means that 1 out of 100 iterations burned the pixel; in odds, that is 1:99 (read as 99-to-1 against burning). Another alternative expression of *BP* is the ratio of the total number of iterations to the number that burned the pixel, expressed as 1-in-X. For a *BP* of 0.01, the result is 1 in 100. It is important to note that the annual likelihood of a wildfire occurring when expressed as 1-in-X trials are not necessarily equivalent to an estimate of the contemporary fire return interval at that point, because these simulations do not address post-fire fuel and vegetation dynamics. In reality, a wildfire occurring this year can affect the likelihood of a wildfire occurring in subsequent years, because the fuelscape is modified. If fires were independent from one year to the next, then the odds would indeed be an estimate of return interval. Because fires are not independent, however, we cannot draw that conclusion. So, an annual *BP* of 0.001 means that the pixel has a 1-in-1000 chance of burning during a fire season, but we cannot conclude that wildfire would occur once every 1000 years.

Annual *BP* varies over several orders of magnitude, so a linear classification with equal intervals does a poor job of classifying *BP* across a landscape. An approximately geometric classification is well-suited for annual *BP* (Table 6). Each class break shown in the table is a factor of 2 or 2.5 times more frequent than the previous class break.

When using a Monte Carlo wildfire occurrence simulation system to quantify *BP*, a burnable pixel may, on occasion, not burn in any iteration, resulting in a *BP* value of zero. Truly non-burnable pixels (open water, bare ground, etc.) also are assigned a *BP* value of zero. On a map, only pixels mapped as non-burnable should be considered to have a *BP* of exactly zero, even if no iterations resulted in a burnable pixel actually burning. It is best to include those "burnable but unburned" pixels in the least-frequent *BP* class.

This discussion of *BP* has referred to a wildfire of any intensity occurring. Both FSim and FlamMap5 can sub-divide the estimate of *BP* by wildfire intensity class. FSim currently partitions *BP* into the six standard FILs (see Table 5). There is no way

Table 6—A scheme for classifying annual burn probability expressed as a decimal fraction, as 1-in-X trials (where X is the inverse of *BP* as a decimal fraction), and as odds. Each class break is 2 to 2.5 times more frequent than the next; every third break is a full order of magnitude (10 times).

Decimal fraction	1-in-X trials	Odds
0.0001	1-in-10,000	1:9999
0.0002	1-in-5000	1:4999
0.0004	1-in-2500	1:2499
0.001	1-in-1000	1:999
0.002	1-in-500	1:499
0.004	1-in-250	1:249
0.01	1-in-100	1:99
0.02	1-in-50	1:49

to reliably infer the type of fire—surface, passive crown, or active crown fire—from these FILs, because fires of all types can produce any of those FILs depending on fuel, weather and topography.

Because flame length is the distinguishing characteristic, *BP* by FIL may also be called flame-length probabilities (*FLP*). In FSim, these FLPs are quantified as conditional probabilities, meaning that they characterize the probability distribution among the FILs given that a wildfire has burned that pixel. The *FLP* values at a pixel sum to 1, and therefore can be used directly as a weighting factor for each FIL, as will be shown in the following section on conditional wildfire intensity.

Tools—Two fire behavior modeling systems—FlamMap5 and FSim—can be used to estimate BP across a landscape. FlamMap5 simulates conditional burn probability—the probability that a pixel will burn given that a wildfire occurs somewhere in the fire modeling landscape. FlamMap's burn probability modeling is typically used to simulate short-duration events occurring during severe weather conditions—the so-called 'problem-fire' scenario. FSim is a more comprehensive *BP* modeling system that produces annual *BP* results by simulating the ignition, growth and suppression of wildfires for tens of thousands of fire seasons. A GIS is essential for developing inputs and generating useful summaries of *BP* simulations.

Conditional Wildfire Intensity

Conditional wildfire intensity is the average intensity of the simulated wildfires that burned the pixel; it inherently incorporates the effects of relative spread direction (heading, flanking, backing, etc.), as well as any effects of variation in wind and fuel moisture, on wildfire intensity. Simply, if a pixel burns 10 times during a simulation, then conditional wildfire intensity is the average wildfire intensity of those 10 wildfires. The total number of iterations does not matter. Conditional wildfire intensity differs from measures of near-maximum wildfire intensity (see previous section) in that it characterizes how variation in weather and spread direction influence the wildfire intensity that occurs, rather than the near-maximum intensity that *could* occur. FlamMap5 and FSim permit calculation of two measures of conditional wildfire intensity: mean fireline intensity (*MFI*) and conditional flame length (*CFL*). Despite their slightly different names and different calculation methods, both attempt to characterize the average wildfire intensity after incorporating variation in relative spread direction, and, when using FSim, variation in wind and fuel moisture.

Mean Fireline Intensity—Mean fireline intensity *(MFI)* is the arithmetic mean fireline intensity of the iterations that actually burned that pixel. *MFI* is calculated directly within FSim as the sum of fireline intensity values for each fire divided by the number of fires that burn the pixel. Although fireline intensity is a more scientifically robust measure of wildfire intensity, it is more difficult to visualize and interpret than flame length due to its complex units (kW/m) and very wide range of variability—more than four orders of magnitude—and therefore is rarely included in a wildfire hazard assessment. Scaling fireline intensity by its common logarithm makes the distribution of values much simpler to interpret. There are two ways to accomplish this scaling. First, the common logarithm of the raw fireline intensity results can be calculated in a GIS, and then a legend for the resulting raster can be created in any convenient way. Second, without taking the common logarithm, the map legend can be generated such that the results fall on a common logarithm scale (Table 4).

USDA Forest Service Gen. Tech. Rep. RMRS-GTR-315. 2013

27

Conditional Flame Length—Conditional flame length (*CFL*) is an estimate of the mean flame length (*FL*) of the iterations that burned the pixel. *CFL* is not calculated directly by FSim or FlamMap5 and must be estimated through an expected value calculation based on the *FLP* values. *CFL* is calculated as the sum-product of *FLP* and flame length across all of the FILs

$$CFL = \sum_{i=1}^{n} FLP_i * FL_i \qquad [4]$$

where FLP_i is the conditional probability of FIL_i and FL_i is the flame length that characterizes FIL_i.

The midpoint of each FIL characterizes flame length for FIL1 through FIL5. A reasonable value must be assigned to FIL6. Table 7 illustrates the calculation of *CFL* for a hypothetical pixel, assuming a 'mid-point' flame length of 7.62 m (25 ft) for FIL6.

Tools—Only two fire behavior modeling systems produce information regarding conditional wildfire intensity—FlamMap5 and FSim. The conditional wildfire intensity outputs generated by FlamMap5 apply to the problem-fire scenario—the typically severe weather conditions that lead to escaped wildfires on the landscape. Although FlamMap5 incorporates non-heading behavior into its simulations of conditional fire intensity, it does not incorporate the possible effects of portions of the landscape burning under less-than-severe conditions that can occur during long-duration wildfires. In contrast, FSim incorporates both non-heading behavior and non-severe weather into its simulations of conditional wildfire intensity.

Conditional flame length is not calculated by either fire behavior modeling system directly, but instead must be calculated using a GIS.

4. HVRA Identification and Characterization

This section addresses a time-consuming but critical step in the overall risk assessment process—the identification and characterization of HVRAs in the study area. Three primary characteristics must be determined for each HVRA identified: spatial extent (mapping), response to wildfire (benefit or loss), and relative importance (Figure 8).

Table 7—Illustration of the calculation of conditional flame length (CFL) from the conditional probability of each fire intensity level occurring and the midpoint flame length of each FIL. There is no midpoint of FIL6, so an arbitrary value must be used. Here, that value is 7.62 m (25 ft).

Fire intensity level (*i*)	Flame-length probability (FLP$_i$)	Mid-point flame length (FL$_i$)	
		- - m - -	- - ft - -
FIL1	0.0	0.33	1
FIL2	0.1	0.91	3
FIL3	0.2	1.52	5
FIL4	0.4	2.13	7
FIL5	0.3	3.05	10
CFL		2.16[a]	7.1

[a] Example: CFL = (0.0×0.33) + (0.1×0.91) + ... + (0.0×7.62) = 2.16 m

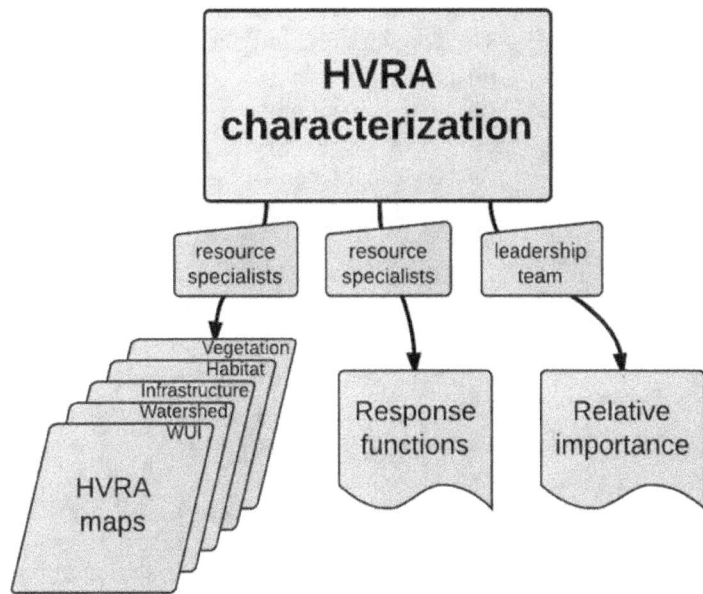

Figure 8—HVRA characterization is a primary component of the overall risk assessment process that produces geospatial data regarding where highly valued resources and assets (HVRAs) are found on the landscape, and tabular data regarding how the HVRAs respond to wildfire as well as their importance relative to one another.

The wildfire hazard results (Section 3) will be combined with the HVRA characteristics described in this section to perform an exposure analysis (Section 5) and an effects analysis (Section 6). This section provides details about the identification and characterization of HVRAs.

HVRA Identification

Identifying which HVRAs to include in the assessment is a critical step in the overall risk assessment process. A key criterion is to limit inclusion of resources and assets to those that are *highly valued*. We recognize mandates for multiple use management and the presence of competing landscape objectives, but nevertheless the scope of analysis may need to be reined in to keep the assessment and interpretation of results manageable. Further, as will become clear later, as more HVRAs are included in the assessment their overall contribution to the weighted risk score will diminish. It is of course possible to perform more refined analyses of specific resources and assets outside of this landscape assessment process.

The HVRA identification process can proceed hierarchically, by first naming primary HVRA categories followed by articulation of a series of sub-HVRAs. For instance, habitat can be the primary HVRA, with sub-HVRAs defined as the habitat for various individual species or species groups. Critical infrastructure is another example, with sub-HVRAs of telecommunication sites, power lines, fire lookouts, etc. Often primary HVRAs will include the wildland urban interface (WUI), other built structures, and municipal watersheds. HVRAs may also be more ecologically oriented and relate to vegetation structure and assemblage. In most cases there will be a range of socioeconomic, natural, and cultural HVRAs included. Quantitatively, all calculations are done at the sub-HVRA level. The hierarchical structure is simply a convenient way to organize and summarize a long list of HVRAs.

Several guiding documents exist to assist in the selection of HVRAs for analysis. The appropriate Land and Resource Management Plan (LRMP; also called a Forest Plan) and Fire Management Plan (FMP)—both of which provide explicit direction on fire management objectives and incident responses—often list resources and assets to protect or enhance. Also, a Wildland Fire Response Guidebook (also called a Forest Response Guidebook) is another useful source of information about resources and assets to protect from wildfire. The process of selecting HVRAs should include consultation with geospatial analysts and resource specialists. Ultimately the selection of which HVRAs to include is determined or approved by the leadership team of the land management unit. Risk to an HVRA cannot be assessed if there is insufficient geospatial data representing the HVRA. Ideally there exists wall-to-wall coverage across the study area with well documented metadata for every HVRA, but that is not always the case. There are a number of geospatial data management issues to address when identifying and mapping HVRAs.

Spatial Extent (Mapping)

For use in wildfire risk calculations, spatial HVRA data, ultimately, needs to be in raster format. Ideally, the raster data should match the extent, cell size and coordinate system of the fire modeling landscape. This may require any of a number of geoprocessing tasks, such as: converting feature class data (points, lines, or polygons) to raster format, re-sampling existing raster-format data to a different cell size, or re-projecting to a different coordinate system. Due to limitations on the spatial accuracy in HVRA mapping and fire modeling, it may be necessary to include a small buffer around point and line features to ensure they are adequately represented in the assessment; it may be undesirable for a point HVRA (a communication site, for example) to be mapped to a single grid cell, especially if the accuracy of the point is small compared to the cell size. Including a buffer size will increase the exposure of the HVRA to wildfire as measured by expected area burned, but otherwise the buffer simply increases the sample size for estimating fire behavior and effects. However, the relative extent factor in the weighted risk calculations counterbalance any increases in mapped HVRA area, so adding a buffer does not bias the overall wildfire threat. The apportionment of relative importance according to the mapped extent of an HVRA not only provides a more equal footing for comparing risk across HVRAs with vastly different spatial extents, but it can also alleviate issues where some HVRAs are mapped much more generously than others, as will be discussed below.

Additional data challenges present themselves in wildfire risk assessments that span administrative and geographic boundaries, including differing data standards used to map HVRAs across adjacent jurisdictions, and distinguishing between data "gaps" and true HVRA absence when combining disparate data sets. Data integration and quality control are essential 'behind the scenes' components of the HVRA characterization process, typically the responsibility of GIS specialists and geospatial analysts in consultation with resource specialists.

The compilation of HVRA data entails collecting data from various sources. Local data sources are often the most up-to-date and reflect local knowledge of the landscape. A variety of regional or national data sources could prove useful, such as certain critical infrastructure layers within the WFDSS, the Forests-to-Faucets dataset for surface drinking water quality, and the SILVIS Lab (Radeloff and others 2005) and Residentially Developed Populated areas (RDPA; Haas and others 2013) datasets for the WUI. LANDFIRE data products are useful for characterizing and mapping vegetation structure and other biophysical variables. Due to the rapidly changing availability and quality of geospatial HVRA data, we will not attempt to catalog all potential sources for all HVRAs.

30

USDA Forest Service Gen. Tech. Rep. RMRS-GTR-315. 2013

The characterization of HVRA susceptibility to wildfire can sometimes be improved by incorporating additional environmental or landscape characteristics. For instance, in past assessments measures of erosion potential such as slope and soil type have been included as variables in response functions for municipal watersheds and aquatic habitat. Though the definition of response functions is a different component, it can be helpful to begin to think through these issues early in the process, and to consider what additional geospatial data may be required.

Although the risk calculations require HVRA data in raster format, any data originally available as a shapefile or feature class should be retained in that format for use in exposure analyses requiring an HVRA to be represented by vector data.

Response to Wildfire

Simulating the response of HVRAs to wildfire is a challenging task subject to substantial uncertainty. Two considerations when characterizing the response of an HVRA to wildfire are (1) the time horizon of the analysis and (2) the notion of HVRA-specific fire effects. The framework represents an assessment of *current* landscape conditions and wildfire risk. Successional processes, disturbances, climate conditions, and a host of other dynamic landscape processes that may take place in the future are not included in this modeling effort; projecting from this assessment to long-term (cumulative) fire effects may not be appropriate. This limitation complicates matters for assessment of ecological fire effects, but does not obviate the importance of including such ecological effects within risk calculations. Similarly, it is inappropriate to define response functions that incorporate future fire risk reduction through fuel treatment effects. Those consequences can be evaluated in future analyses with updated fuel conditions, or in a comparative framework to analyze fuel treatment scenarios. Rather, response functions are designed to target the susceptibility of individual HVRAs to fire effects—the bottom leg of the risk triangle—not likelihood or intensity (Figure 1). Simply put, this framework can be used to monitor, but not model, temporal trends in wildfire risk.

The response function framework we describe here requires quantifying the relationship between HVRA-value and wildfire intensity (measured by flame length). We relate HVRA response to fire intensity because it is the best fire characteristic available for relating to fire effects, and because it integrates two important fire characteristics—fuel consumption and spread rate. This approach quantifies net value change (NVC) to a given HVRA as the percentage change in the initial resource value resulting from a fire at a given intensity. Response functions address relative rather than absolute change in resource or asset value, and represent both beneficial and adverse effects to the HVRA. It is possible to incorporate additional variables into response functions, subject to the quality and availability of spatial data to map the additional variables. For instance, in previous analyses impacts to watersheds were differentiated according to factors influencing post-fire erosion risk (Thompson and others 2013a, b). More in-depth analysis could consider additional modeling to augment or substitute for response function definitions, for instance fire effects on tree mortality (Ager and others 2007, 2010) or post-fire debris flow modeling (Cannon and others 2010).

The approach we promote here is based on using the best judgment of experts as a substitute for mathematical fire effects models, which may be inadequate, difficult to parameterize, or nonexistent (Hyde and others 2013). Typically, this elicitation will occur in a workshop setting, and incorporates input and feedback from several individuals. Factors influencing implementation of expert-based approaches include identification of: the type of information to be elicited, the most appropriate experts, and the best way to encapsulate and elicit expert information. Further driving many applications are practical considerations relating to available resources and timelines. Below we outline an eight-step process for eliciting expert judgment, premised largely on frameworks presented by Knol and others (2010), Kuhnert and others (2010), and MacMillan and Marshall (2006). The process employs multiple experts, seeks expert consensus, and provides multiple opportunities to refine HVRA-specific response function definitions.

Step 1: Articulate the Research Question—Articulation of the research question will frame the study design, the collection and aggregation of relevant data, and ultimately the structure of the modeling approach. The research question in the wildfire context is how to characterize wildfire effects to HVRAs, and how to integrate that information with wildfire simulation modeling outputs in order to characterize wildfire risk. To align with the wildfire risk assessment framework of Finney (2005), characterization of fire effects should be both spatially explicit and quantitative.

Step 2: Identify and Characterize Relevant Uncertainties—Identifying and characterizing uncertainties affect choices about the type of information to elicit, the type of experts to engage, and the format of the elicitation. Formally identifying and characterizing the uncertainties can prove very useful for distinguishing between the types of uncertainties faced and for identifying appropriate approaches for managing uncertainty (Ascough and others 2008; Thompson and Calkin 2011). Limited understanding of fire effects can be a key source of knowledge uncertainty in the wildfire management context. This type of uncertainty can be best managed with expert input as opposed to, say, variability in fire occurrence and spread, which is better managed with probabilistic wildfire modeling.

Step 3: Resolve the Scope and Format of Elicitation—This step entails identification of the number of experts to engage and the nature of the engagement (interview, group workshop, survey distribution, etc.), while considering available resources and other constraints. Due to time constraints, a one- or two-day group workshop is appropriate. Establishment of expert sub-groups based upon alignment of relevant expertise with HVRA and sub-HVRA layers, where feasible, is recommended.

Step 4: Select the Expert(s)—Given the choice to employ multiple experts (Step 3), the task in this step becomes identification of the appropriate type and balance of experts, given availability and other constraints. Types of experts can include generalists, subject-matter experts, and process experts. In this context, generalists span a range of professions, including fire management officers, fuels specialists, fire planners, foresters, silviculturists, and district rangers. Specialists, by contrast, are HVRA-specific, including wildlife biologists, fisheries biologists, soil scientists, and forest hydrologists. Process experts have experience in risk assessment and group facilitation.

Step 5: Design the Expert Judgment Elicitation Protocol—Protocol design considers the intended use of the elicited information, how to best encapsulate that information, and how to best elicit that information. In this context, HVRA-specific response functions output net value change as a function of fire intensity and potentially other spatial variables. These response functions are then used to summarize risk across the landscape and across HVRAs (see Equations 1 and 2).

Step 6: Prepare the Elicitation Protocol—A key component to preparing for expert elicitation is the provision of background information to experts. This background information should outline the issue at hand, identify relevant uncertainties, and provide details about the elicitation procedure. Informative brochures that introduce and outline the process can be useful. It can also be useful to distribute surveys to experts ahead of time to inquire about factors affecting how each HVRA responded to wildfire, and to prime the pump, so to speak. One such survey used in the past queried experts regarding three key factors: wildfire characteristics, HVRA characteristics, and landscape characteristics. The surveys served to introduce experts to the mental process of evaluating fire effects, and further to help identify potential variables to include in response function definitions.

Step 7: Elicit Expert Judgment—As previously described, the elicitation protocol presented here is based around a group workshop format, and involves multiple individuals that can vary by nature of expertise (generalist and subject-matter experts). The workshop is premised on consensus-based definition of quantitative HVRA-specific response functions. The workshops typically begin by reviewing the definition of HVRA layers, the initial feedback from survey responses, and the role of response functions in the risk assessment framework. Then the process of assigning response functions can proceed, and, if applicable, the group can be broken down according to HVRA subgroups. Including documentation for rationales behind response functions is a critical piece of information. This documentation can include references to published literature, other models, and observations, in addition to expert opinion.

Step 8: Provide Feedback and Refine—Post-elicitation feedback provides an opportunity for critique and evaluation from the larger group of experts, can encourage reflection of engaged experts, and allows for iterative revision or refinement of stated expert judgment. This process will begin by having experts present their response function definitions and justifications, followed by critique and debate, and where appropriate, modification of response function definitions.

There exist other approaches, which in some cases seek to explicitly quantify the level of agreement or disagreement between experts (Marcot and others 2012). There also exist a multitude of tools, datasets, and other sources that experts can turn to for help in thinking through response function definitions. Peterson and others (2007) provide an extensive list, including the Fire Effects Information System (FEIS), CONSUME, the First Order Effects Fire Model (FOFEM), the Fire and Fuels Extension–Forest Vegetation Simulator (FFE-FVS), and the Wildlife Habitat Response Model (WHRM). Selection of the appropriate framework for eliciting and encapsulating expert opinion, and more broadly for characterizing fire effects, will vary by planning context and assessment needs.

Relative Importance

Balancing competing or conflicting land and resource management objectives is a significant challenge to land and resource management planners. Likewise, it is also difficult to articulate quantitative weights establishing the relative importance of HVRAs. This step is not necessary when assessing wildfire risk to a single HVRA such as municipal watersheds or the WUI. It is only when attempting to combine the risk to multiple overlapping HVRAs, or when comparing risk among several HVRAs, that the issue of weighting arises. Even then, the task can be avoided altogether by assuming that each pixel of each HVRA is of equal value, or weight. With that assumption, however, over-mapping an HVRA will overstate its risk, and extensive HVRAs will always be shown to have greater effects than HVRAs that cover a small amount of land area. There are some strong tradeoffs to consider before avoiding the step of articulating relative importance. Without relative importance, how does one characterize risk in areas where multiple HVRAs overlap? How does one compare risks across different spatial areas that house different HVRAs? Using relative importance scores helps to address all of these questions, and allows for summarization and visualization of risks in a single metric. Further, if assessment results are to ultimately be used for planning mitigation treatments and strategies, then prioritization decisions that integrate all HVRAs will still ultimately need to be made. Articulating relative importance scores and how objectives are balanced makes this decision explicit rather than implicit, and increases the overall transparency of decision processes (Marcot and others 2012).

There are a number of places to turn for guidance in articulating relative importance scores, with which leadership will likely be well familiar. These include the USDA Strategic Plan, the USDA Forest Service Strategic Plan, national fire policy documents, regional restoration strategies, LRMPs, FMPs, and a host of other documents, regulations and laws. Principally LRMPs and FMPs will contain the most location-specific information on HVRAs and management objectives.

As with response function definition, a workshop is a recommended setting for eliciting relative importance. The purpose of this workshop is to establish quantitative weights that differentiate the importance of HVRAs and sub-HVRAs. Absent the ability to work closely with a resource economist (or team of economists) to monetize all HVRAs, the use of multi-criteria decision analysis is recommended. Below we present a type of multi-criteria decision analysis that is effectively the Simple Multi-Attribute Rating Technique, or SMART (Kajanus and others 2004), although a variety of other multi-criteria decision analysis techniques could be used (Ananda and Herath 2009). Relative importance weights are assigned according to a three-step process (below), which proceeds first across HVRA categories, and then hierarchically across sub-HVRAs within an HVRA category. Rank HVRAs and sub-HVRAs according to importance to the group conducting the assessment.

1. Provide qualitative justification for rankings, and their relation to existing guidance/doctrine/policy.
2. Assign top-ranked HVRA and sub-HVRA a score of 100; assign all other HVRAs and sub-HVRAs relative importance scores on scale of 0-100. Relative importance scores can also be converted into percentages of overall importance across HVRAs and across sub-HVRAs within a given HVRA category.
3. Review, critique, and refine scores (iterative for both HVRAs and sub-HVRAs).

Effects analysis is conducted at the pixel level, so the weighting for relative importance of each HVRA must, ultimately, also pertain to a unit area. However, it is easier to first elucidate the importance of an HVRA as a whole, as described above, and then divide by its extent. The relative importance score for a particular HVRA is spread evenly over all pixels of that HVRA for use in the effects analysis calculations. Thus, for HVRAs with a very broad extent, the relative importance per individual pixel might be very low; for less extensive HVRAs the relative importance per pixel might be very high.

Consider a stylized example landscape with two HVRAs (Communication sites and Watersheds). The Communication Sites HVRA, taken as a whole, has been assigned a relative importance of 50 percent of Watersheds HVRA, meaning that two-thirds of the overall importance (100/150) is allocated to watersheds and the remaining one-third to Communication sites (Table 8). The communication sites HVRA covers a relatively small land area compared to the watersheds HVRA, meaning that it has a smaller relative extent (*RE*). In our framework, the relative importance is distributed across each

Table 8—Hypothetical example of the relative importance (RI) and relative extent (RE) calculations. The ratio of RI to RE is used as a weighting factor when combining HVRA results.

HVRA	Relative importance (RI)	Share of importance (percent)	Relative extent (RE)	RI/RE
Communication sites	50	33.3	2	25
Watersheds	100	66.7	100	1

HVRAs extent, so RI divided by RE is the appropriate weighting factor. Ultimately, the *RI/RE* in this example is greatest for the communication sites because they cover so little land area. In contrast, a unit area of watershed has just 1/25th the importance per unit area of the communication sites, despite the fact that watersheds, taken as a whole, were assigned twice the importance of the communication sites.

5. Exposure Analysis

Exposure analysis is the characterization of wildfire likelihood and intensity where HVRAs occur (Figure 9). Modeling of wildfire likelihood and intensity was covered in Section 3; identifying where HVRAs occur—their spatial extent—was covered in Section 4. Exposure analysis can be performed within a GIS using one of several geospatial techniques that identify or summarize the wildfire hazard characteristics of all pixels where an HVRA is mapped (a 'Sample' in ESRI's ArcMap), or a calculation of descriptive statistics that summarize the hazard characteristics ('Zonal Stats' in ArcMap). The ArcFuels Toolbar for ArcMap (Vaillant and others 2013) also performs these functions.

In an exposure analysis, wildfire hazard can be characterized for an HVRA using several different summaries. First, a histogram or box plot of a wildfire hazard characteristic—*BP*, *MFI* and *CFL* are common measures in an exposure analysis—illustrates the distribution of these characteristics across the HVRA or within specific units of an HVRA. For example, Scott and others (2012b) compared box plots of *BP*, *MFI* and integrated wildfire hazard (the product of *BP* and *MFI*) for ten municipal watersheds on the Beaverhead-Deerlodge National Forest, Montana (Figure 10).

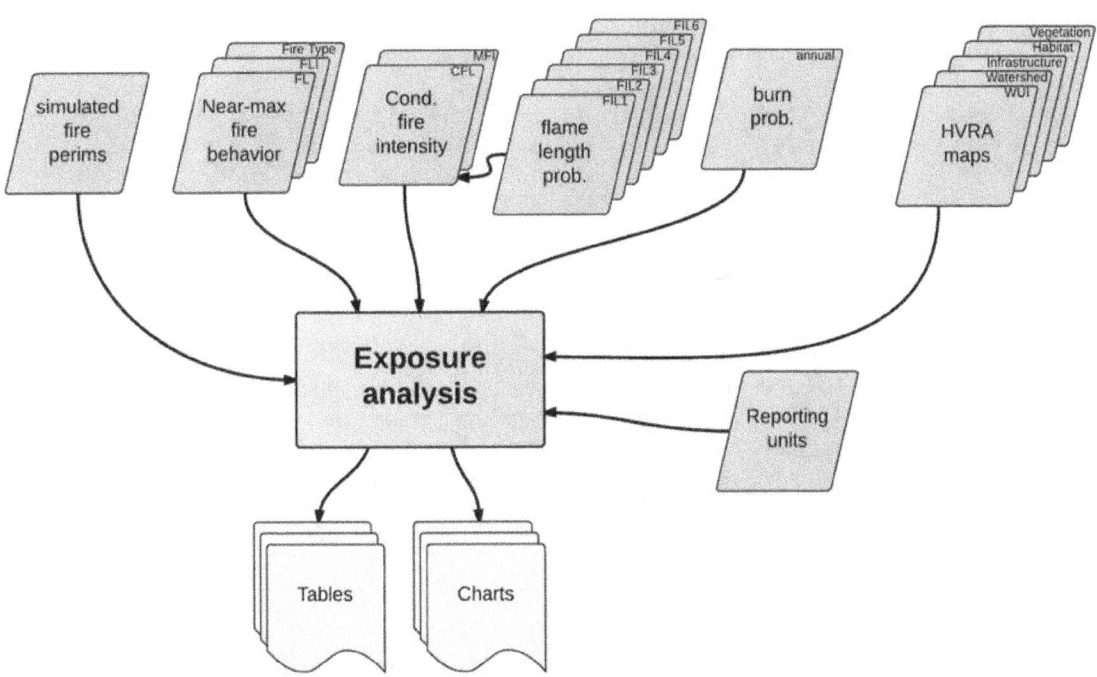

Figure 9—The exposure analysis component of the overall wildfire risk assessment process uses outputs from the wildfire simulation and HVRA characterization components to generate tabular and graphical summaries of wildfire characteristics where HVRAs occur, optionally summarized by reporting units. A reporting unit is an administrative unit (Forest or Ranger District, for example) or other geographic area such as a hydrologic unit.

USDA Forest Service Gen. Tech. Rep. RMRS-GTR-315. 2013

35

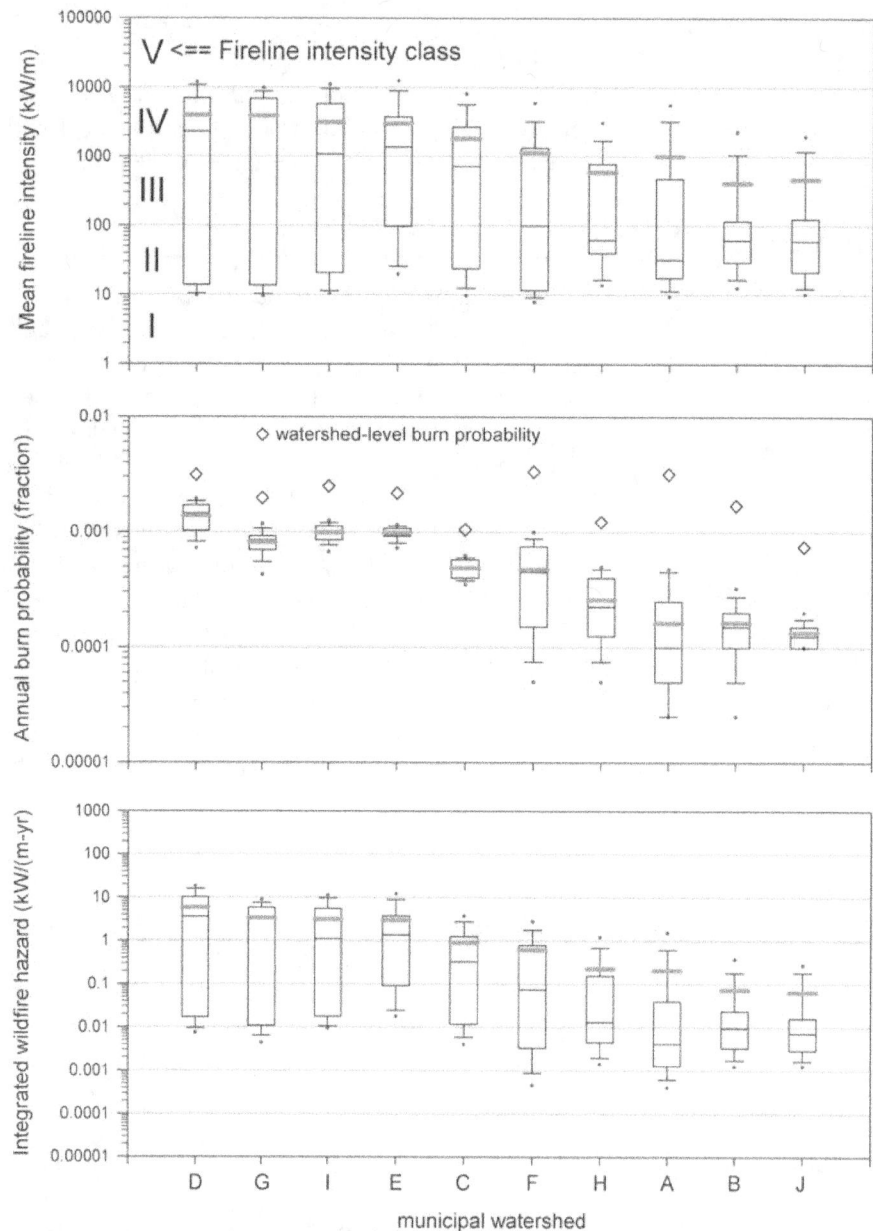

Figure 10—Box plots of BP, MFI, and integrated hazard (BP * MFI) for all 10 municipal watersheds, sorted by mean integrated hazard. Box plots indicate the quartiles (the box), 10th/90th percentiles (whiskers), median (black line), mean (thick grey line), and individual values outside the 10th/90th percentiles (dots). The BP box plots also indicate the probability that a wildfire will reach any portion of the watershed (diamond) (reproduced from Scott and others 2012b).

Because integrated wildfire hazard is $BP \times MFI$, it is amenable to being plotted on a single chart as a scatterplot, with reference lines delineating zones of equal integrated hazard. Because BP and MFI can vary over several orders of magnitude, it may be convenient to generate this plot on a log-log scale, as Scott and others (2012b) did for two contrasting watersheds (Figure 11). Such scatterplots are particularly useful for identifying HVRAs with a greater tendency to experience fire or to experience fire of a given intensity level (Ager and others 2012).

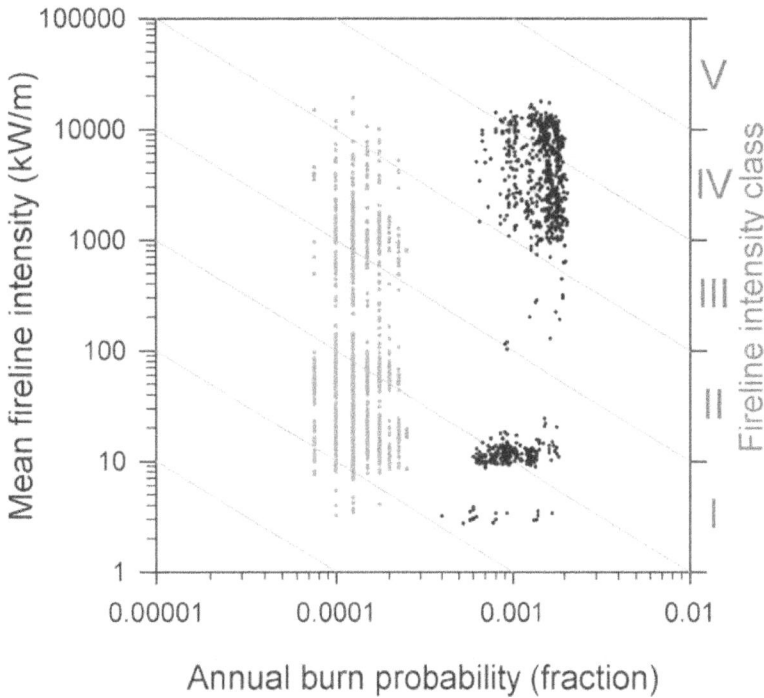

Figure 11—Wildfire hazard characteristics chart for two contrasting municipal watersheds. Gray dots represent the watershed with the lowest integrated hazard; black dots represent the watershed with the highest integrated hazard (reproduced from Scott and others 2012b).

Expected annual HVRA area burned is another characteristic that can be identified during an assessment of HVRA exposure to wildfire. Expected annual HVRA area burned is calculated as the product of HVRA-mean *BP* and burnable HVRA area; it represents the average amount of HVRA area burned in the wildfire simulations. Expected annual watershed area burned for the example of municipal watersheds is shown in Table 9.

6. Effects Analysis

Effects analysis integrates wildfire hazard (likelihood and intensity) and HVRA vulnerability (exposure and susceptibility), producing a comprehensive measure of wildfire risk (Figure 12). We quantify wildfire risk as the weighted expectation of net value change [E(*wNVC*)], where *NVC* is expressed in relative terms on a percentage basis, as defined by expert-based loss/benefit functions (for example, complete loss = -100 percent). The ArcFuels Toolbar for ArcMap (Vaillant and others 2013) provides some functionality for applying response functions.

A given pixel on the landscape can present risk to multiple HVRAs. Equation 1 provided the formula for calculating E*(NVC)* for a single pixel of a single HVRA. To provide an integrated measure of wildfire risk across multiple HVRAs, a weighting scheme that includes the relative importance (RI_j) and relative extent (RE_j) of each HVRA must be incorporated; this formulation was presented in Equation 2. The overall relative importance score (RI_j), which applies to the HVRA as a whole, is divided by RE_j in order to allocate the importance across the area where the HVRA occurs. Incorporating the relative extent of HVRAs (for example, number of grid cells covered by the HVRA) distributes relative importance across HVRAs with a large number of mapped pixels HVRAs with few mapped pixels can have a high importance per pixel even if their overall importance is not high.

USDA Forest Service Gen. Tech. Rep. RMRS-GTR-315. 2013

37

Table 9—Summary of pixel-based wildfire hazard characteristics within each of the ten municipal watersheds on the Beaverhead-Deerlodge National Forest. Expected annual area burned (column d) is the product of watershed-mean burn probability (column b) and the burnable watershed area (column c). Expected annual area burned as a fraction of the burnable watershed area is therefore equivalent to the watershed-mean burn probability (adapted from Scott and others (2012b).

(a)	(b)	(c)	(d)
Watershed	Mean burn probability	Burnable watershed area	Expected annual area burned
		ha	ha/yr
A	0.0001628	10,093	1.64
B	0.0001634	3,115	0.51
C	0.0004873	521	0.25
D	0.0013794	722	1.00
E	0.0009767	2,494	2.44
F	0.0004720	5,930	2.80
G	0.0008151	1,580	1.29
H	0.0002570	1,264	0.32
I	0.0009899	1,303	1.29
J	0.0001347	1,330	0.18

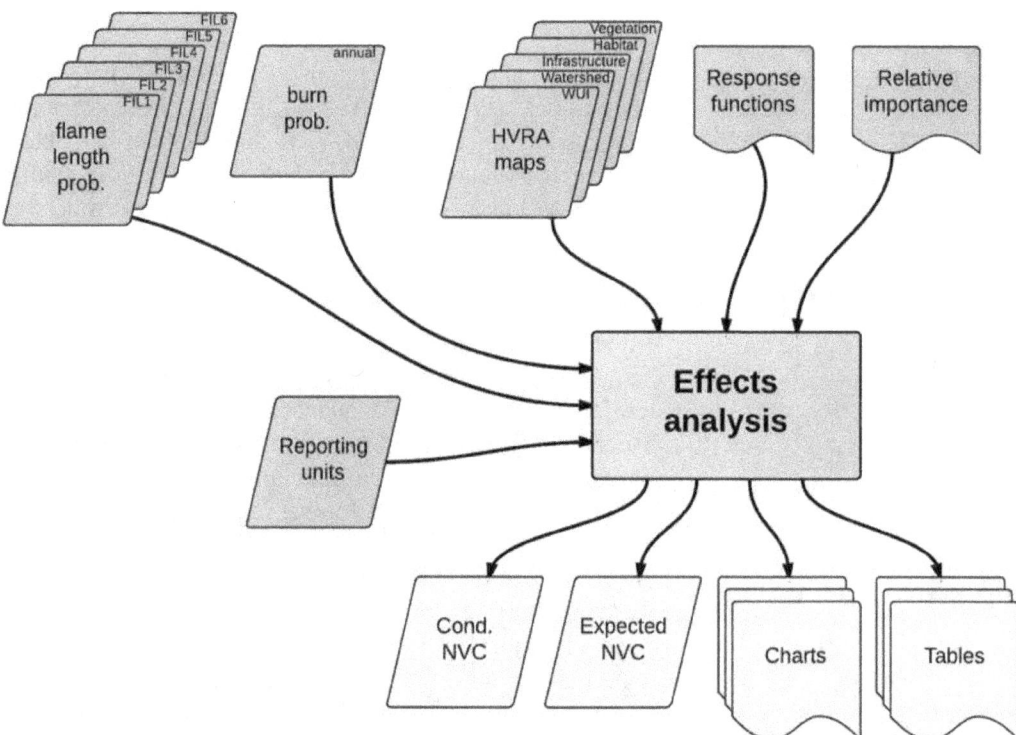

Figure 12—The effects analysis component of the overall risk assessment process draws from outputs from wildfire simulation and HVRA characterization components to produce the most comprehensive measures of wildfire risk. Like the exposure analysis, the effects analysis results can be summarized by reporting units. A reporting unit is an administrative unit (forest or ranger district, for example) or other geographic area such as a hydrologic unit.

38

USDA Forest Service Gen. Tech. Rep. RMRS-GTR-315. 2013

7. Interpreted Example: Bridger-Teton National Forest_____

In this section we will illustrate each component of a comprehensive geospatial wildfire risk assessment conducted for the Bridger-Teton National Forest (BTNF), located in far western Wyoming. This example application originated from the Tetons Interagency Risk Assessment (TIARA), an interagency assessment of wildfire risk to HVRAs within Grand Teton National Park and the BTNF (Scott and others 2013). In that assessment, each agency first identified a suite of HVRAs to be analyzed, and then characterized the susceptibility and relative importance of those HVRAs according to the assessment process outlined by Thompson and others (2013a). For simplicity, this example focuses on the BTNF portion of the assessment.

A wide range of fuel types, biophysical settings, and vegetation types occur within the 3.5 million acre BTNF. The valley-bottoms, at roughly 2,000 m elevation, are covered by grasslands and grass mixed with sagebrush (*Artemisia tridentata*). The highest peaks in the study area exceed 3,600 m; the terrain above 3,000 m typically does not support wildfire spread due to the prevalence of rock and persistent snow. The slopes between the valley-bottoms and the peaks are covered by coniferous forests, montane meadows, and stands dominated by quaking aspen (*Populous tremuloides*).

Wildfire Simulation

Fire Modeling Landscape—For the assessment, we used LFDAT to download and process LANDFIRE version 1.0.5 (Refresh 2001) datasets of fuel, vegetation, and topography. The landscape extent included a minimum buffer of 10 miles from the National Forest and National Park administrative boundaries (Figure 13). This buffer allows for the simulation of wildfire spread onto the study area from adjacent land without introducing an artificial "edge effect." Using LFTFC, we worked with local resource specialists to critique and update vegetation characteristics and the associated surface fire behavior fuel model mapping rules. We also updated the fire modeling landscape to reflect wildfire and insect disturbance for the time period of 2001 through 2010. The end result is a fire modeling landscape current as of the 2011 fire season.

A summary of surface and canopy fuel characteristics was made by finding the unique combinations of fuel model, canopy base height, canopy bulk density, canopy cover, and vegetation system group physiology (hereafter called vegetation system). Vegetation system is an attribute of LANDFIRE's Existing Vegetation Type dataset, and reflects the type of vegetation currently present at each landscape pixel. Pivot tables were used to summarize the distribution of land area covered by different surface fire behavior fuel models (Scott and Burgan 2005) among the various vegetation systems, in three separate tables: non-burnable areas (Table 10), which comprise 10 percent of the landscape; burnable areas with no overlying forest canopy (Table 11), which comprise 54 percent of the entire landscape; and burnable areas with a forest canopy present (Table 12), which comprise 36 percent of the entire landscape. The areas mapped to fuel model NB9 (bare ground) in the grassland and shrubland vegetation systems occur because the fuel conditions in those areas do not support fire spread; they were found primarily high in the mountains adjacent to non-vegetated systems.

Burnable areas with no forest canopy were identified as burnable pixels where canopy cover = 0. Fuel models GR1, GS2, and SH1 cover more than 80 percent of such areas; GS2 alone covers 41 percent of the burnable non-forested area (Table 11). Similarly, TU1 and TL3 cover 62 percent of the forested portion of the landscape, and TU1 alone covers 41 percent (Table 12). Less than 10 percent of the forested landscape is covered by TU5.

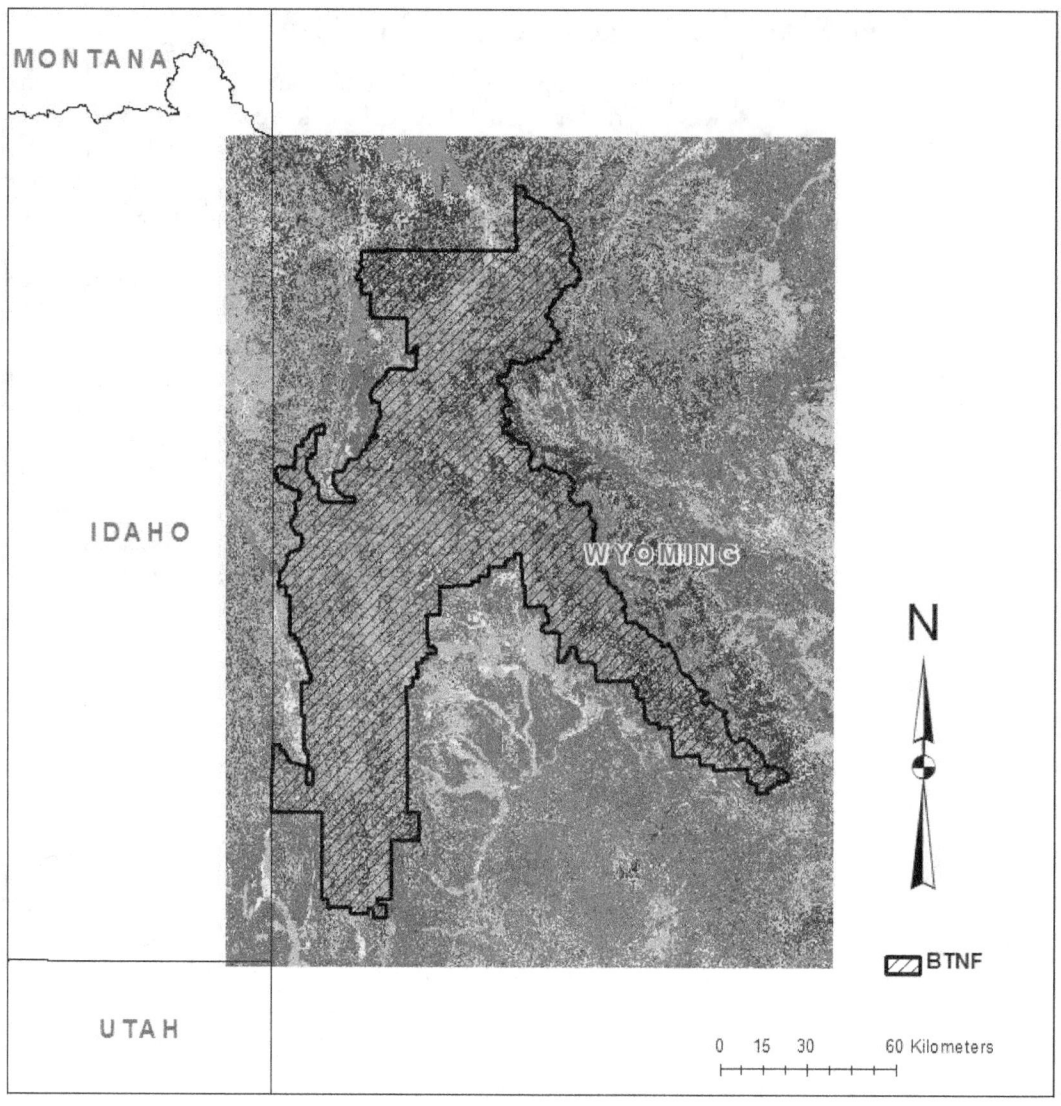

Figure 13—Overview of the 5.8 million ha (14.4 million acre) Teton Interagency Risk Assessment landscape (rectangle in center of figure). The study area includes the Bridger-Teton National Forest (shown in crosshatch) and Grand Teton National Park, plus a minimum buffer of 16 km (10 mi).

Table 10—Distribution of land area (ha) covered by non-burnable fuel models (Scott and Burgan 2005) by vegetation system on the Teton Interagency Risk Assessment landscape. Ten percent of the entire landscape is non-burnable. Fuel model NB1 refers to developed urban areas that cannot support wildfire spread' NB2 refers to permanent snowfields or glaciers; NB3 refers to non-burnable agricultural land; NB8 refers to open water; and NB9 refers to land with insufficient wildland fuel to support wildfire spread.

Fuel model		Agricultural	Developed	Non-vegetated	Sparsely vegetated	Grassland	Shrubland	Total
		- hectares -						
NB1	Urban		16,226					16,226
NB2	Snow/ice			7,130				7,130
NB3	Agricultural	169,452						169,452
NB8	Open water			71,941				71,941
NB9	Bare ground		600	82,270	11,605	213,357	7,084	314,916
	TOTAL	169,452	16,826	161,341	11,605	213,357	7,084	579,665

USDA Forest Service Gen. Tech. Rep. RMRS-GTR-315. 2013

Table 11—Distribution of land area (ha) by fuel model (Scott and Burgan 2005) and vegetation system for areas with no overlying forest canopy cover on the Teton Interagency Risk Assessment fire modeling landscape (54 percent of the landscape).

Fuel model	Agricultural	Developed	Grassland	Exotic herbaceous	Shrubland	Exotic tree-shrub	Hard-wood	Riparian	Conifer	Total
					- - hectares - -					
GR1	684		321,121	33,127	266,449				171	621,553
GR2	9,832		148,650	1,247	237				236	160,204
GR4					2					2
GS1		11,325	488		80,797				369	92,977
GS2			11		1,286,930				286	1,287,228
SH1					641,599					641,599
SH2					155,998		19	1,538	436	157,991
SH5						1,160				1,160
SH7					61	714			230	1,005
TU1								67,722	5	67,726
TL1			76,401							76,423
TL3					58,120				55	58,175
TL8									30	30
SUM	10,517	11,325	546,672	34,375	2,490,213	1,874	19	69,260	1,817	3,166,071

USDA Forest Service Gen. Tech. Rep. RMRS-GTR-315. 2013

41

Table 12—Distribution of land area (ha) by fuel model (Scott and Burgan 2005) and vegetation type for areas with an overlying forest canopy (36 percent of the Teton Interagency Risk Assessment landscape).

FBFM	Developed	Conifer-hardwood	Hardwood	Riparian	Conifer	Grand total
GR1		102	4		165,154	165,260
GR2				116	17	133
GS1		1,620		166	321	947
GS2		130		40,672	50,743	91,544
SH1		117				117
SH2		21,634			16,381	38,015
SH7					151	151
TU1	890	67,983	195,167	38,435	549,505	851,981
TU2		2,437			154,358	156,795
TU5		11,807			155,928	167,735
TL1		195	640		3,990	4,825
TL3			4		425,871	425,875
TL4			645		102,191	102,835
TL5					63,396	63,396
TL6	1,751					1,751
SUM	2,641	105,025	196,460	79,229	1,688,005	2,071,360

Summary statistics were calculated for canopy base height and canopy bulk density in the forested areas of the landscape. Canopy base height averaged 2.0 m across the forested landscape, but averaged 1.4 m in the conifer vegetation types and 1.5 m in the conifer-hardwood types (Table 13). Canopy bulk density averaged 0.06 kg/m^3 across the forested landscape, but was slightly higher in the conifer types; the maximum canopy bulk density (0.45 kg/m^3) also occurred in the conifer vegetation types (Table 13).

The fuel and vegetation rasters were generated using LFTFC, then a fire modeling landscape file (LCP) was generated from these fuel and vegetation layers, plus slope, aspect, and elevation rasters, using LFDAT.

Historical Weather—In this section we illustrate a few basic summaries of the historical weather information gathered for the TIARA: (1) percentile values of *ERC-G* and 1-hr moisture content (*MC*), (2) Seasonal *ERC-G* chart, and (3) 6-m (20-ft) wind speed and direction.

Table 13—Summary statistics for canopy fuel characteristics (canopy base height and canopy bulk density) in forested areas of the landscape.

				Cover type			
	Statistic	Developed	Conifer/hard-wood	Hard-wood	Riparian	Conifer	Land-scape mean
canopy base height (m)	Min	2.0	0.4	1.6	0.1	0.0	0.0
	Mean	3.1	1.5	7.2	2.8	1.4	2.0
	Max	4.9	10.0	10.0	10.0	10.0	10.0
canopy bulk density (kg/m^3)	Min	0.01	0.01	0.01	0.01	0.01	0.01
	Mean	0.06	0.06	0.01	0.05	0.07	0.06
	Max	0.08	0.30	0.01	0.34	0.45	0.45

After evaluating several weather stations, we selected the Raspberry RAWS as most representative of the entire landscape because it was somewhat centrally located, its ridgetop location was not subject to valley-influenced wind directions, and its elevation was more representative of the landscape than most other RAWS, which tended to be located in the valley bottoms. All of the summaries presented in this section were made from information contained in the so-called 'FRISK file' (for 'fire risk') generated by the FlamMap Fire Risk Export feature of FireFamily Plus. The fire danger fuel model at Raspberry RAWS was already set to fuel model G, so no adjustment was necessary. Before generating the FRISK file we replaced the 10-minute average wind speed in the database with the probable maximum 1-minute average with an update query using database management software. From the FRISK file we identified a few percentile values of *ERC-G* and dead 1-h fuel moisture content (Table 14).

These percentile values are useful both on their own and for generating the remaining weather summaries. In the near-maximum fire behavior section below it will be necessary to know the 97th percentile dead fuel moisture content values for all three size classes of dead surface fuel. From the same FRISK file, the 97th percentile 10-h timelag moisture content value was determined to be 4 percent, and the 100-h timelag moisture content was 8 percent.

Figure 14 depicts the seasonal trend in *ERC-G* at the weather station. Both the daily mean value and the mean plus two standard deviations are shown, with the 80th, 90th and 97th percentile *ERC-G* values indicated. Note that the mean *ERC-G* value barely reaches the 80th percentile value even at its highest.

Table 14—Percentile values of ERC-G and dead 1-h timelag moisture content as determined from the FRISK file for the Raspberry RAWS, 1999-2010.

Percentile	ERC-G	Dead 1-h timelag moisture content (percent)
80th	49	5.0
90th	56	4.2
97th	69	2.9

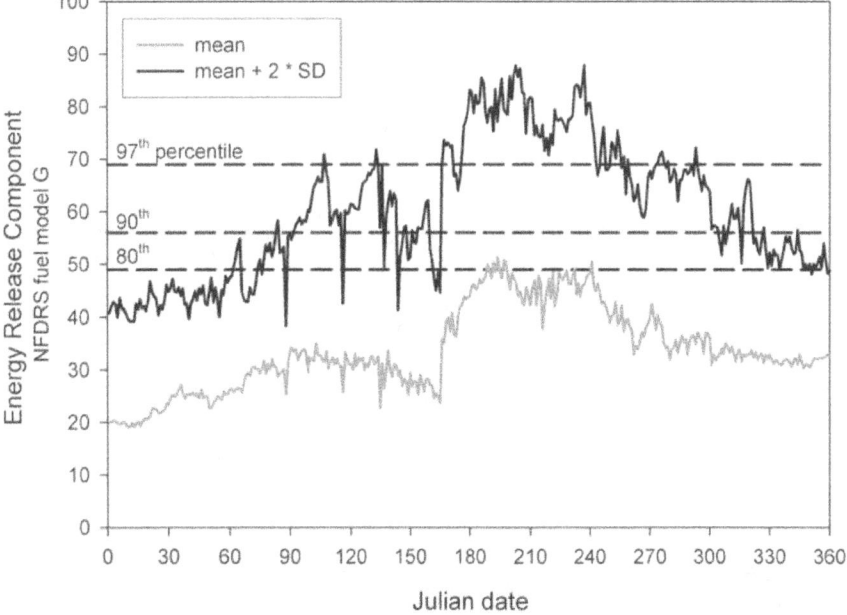

Figure 14—Seasonal trend in daily mean ERC-G and mean plus two standard deviations for the Raspberry RAWS, as calculated in FireFamily Plus and summarized in the FRISK file (data years 1990 – 2010). For reference, the 80th, 90th, and 97th percentile values of ERC-G (see Table 14) are shown.

The next summary from the FRISK file is the joint distribution of wind speed and direction. Such joint distributions are most often displayed as a wind rose (Figure 15). The wind rose is an excellent chart for showing the dominance of wind direction, but can be challenging to use for judging the relative frequency of wind speed.

Mathematical models capable of adapting the landscape-average wind speed and direction (or the wind speed and direction at a specific point on the landscape) to wind speed and direction across an entire landscape based on topography and vegetation cover—Wind Wizard and Wind Ninja—are now available. The use of such terrain-adapted winds has proven useful for simulating fire growth using the FARSITE and FlamMap5 systems, as well as within WFDSS. However, their application in wildfire hazard assessment is challenging. Two wildfire hazard modeling applications could potentially use terrain-adapted winds: modeling burn probability and conditional fire intensity using Monte Carlo simulation, and modeling the near-maximum potential wildfire behavior. The FSim fire occurrence and growth simulation system could theoretically use terrain-adapted winds, but it currently does not have that capability—it would need more than 40 wind simulations, one for each combination of wind speed and direction. Using terrain-adapted winds for modeling near-maximum fire potential is problematic because, unless all directions are simulated, the selected wind direction may result in far lower than maximum wind speeds on certain aspects

For simulating the near-maximum fire behavior it will be necessary to estimate the 97th percentile 6-m (20-ft) wind speed (probable maximum 1-minute average) occurring during the typical burning period of the typical fire season. This was estimated by

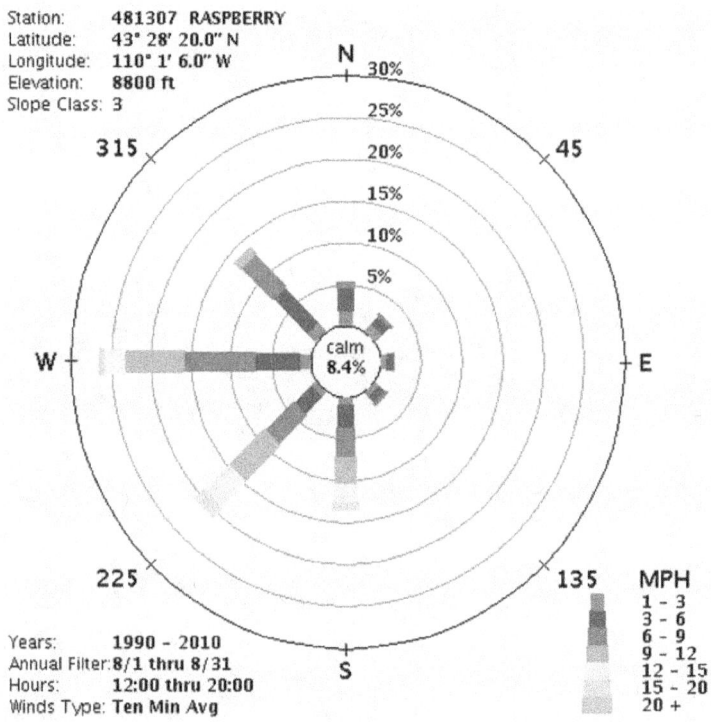

Figure 15—Wind rose constructed from the joint distribution wind speed and direction during the calendar month of August, 1200 – 2000 hours, at the Raspberry RAWS (data years 1990 – 2010). The wind rose clearly shows the relative frequency of wind directions, but does not indicate the relative frequency of wind speeds well.

generating a daily listing of the probable maximum 1-min average wind speed for every day of the hourly data record (1990-2010 in this case). In Excel, the dataset was filtered to include only the months May – October and only the hours between noon and 8 pm. The 97th percentile value was calculated from this filtered dataset. The result was 32 km/h (20 mi/hr). This wind speed was exceeded only 3 percent of the time during the historical period (within the fire season months and burn period hours).

Historical Fire Occurrence—Three summaries illustrate historical fire occurrence within the TIARA fire modeling landscape. The first fire occurrence summary is a set of charts showing the acres burned by wildfires of different sizes. Figure 16 plots the cumulative land area burned over the historical period (normalized so that the total land area burned = 100) against the cumulative number of fires during the period, sorted from smallest to largest. Line coloring indicates fire size class. Size class A and B fires (fires up to 4 ha final size) account for almost 90 percent of all fires, but less than 1 percent of the land area burned. The large black dots on the chart indicate the land area burned by fires of the 90th, 95th, 98th, and 99th percentiles by size; those results are also tabulated in Table 15. A pair of histograms—one for number of fires and another for acres burned—also shows the asymmetrical distribution of the number of fires and area burned by fires of different size classes (Figure 17).

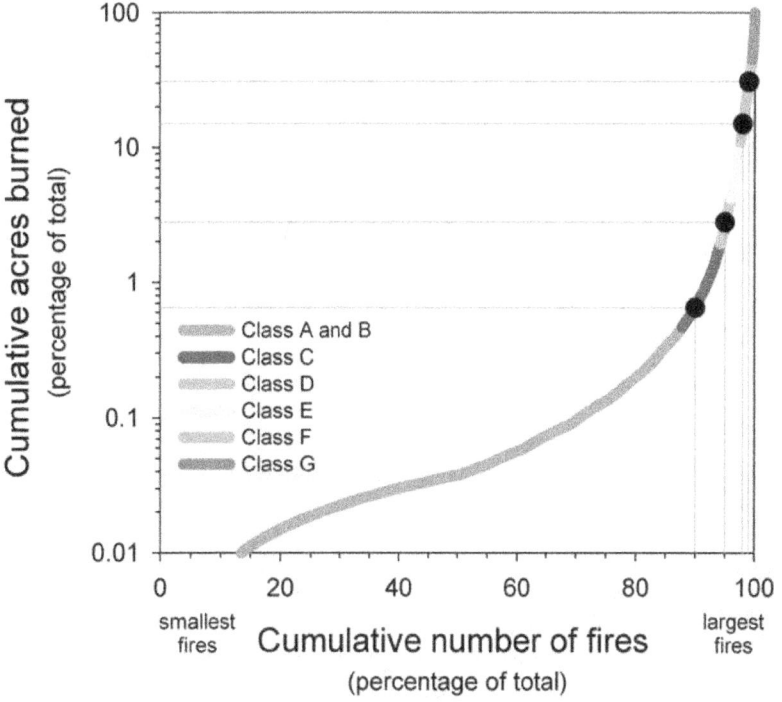

Figure 16—Cumulative number of historical fires on the X-axis (sorted from smallest to largest and expressed as a percentage of the total number of historical fires) versus historical cumulative acres burned (as a percentage of total) on the Y-axis (log scale) by fire size class. Black dots indicate the 90th, 95th, 97th and 99th percentile fires. The smallest 90 percent of the historical fires (those less than 6 ha [15 ac]) accounted for less than 1 percent of the acres burned, and the smallest 99 percent of fires (those less than 1214 ha [3000 ac]) accounted for just 31 percent of the total acres burned. Class A and B = fires less than 4 ha final size; Class C = 4 – 40 ha; Class D = 40 – 121 ha; Class E = 121 – 404 ha; Class F = 404 – 2023 ha; Class G = fires larger than 2023 ha.

USDA Forest Service Gen. Tech. Rep. RMRS-GTR-315. 2013

45

Table 15—Fraction of historical acres burned by wildfires larger than the given percentile size. These results indicate the strongly non-linear influence of large fires on area burned (and therefore burn probability).

Percentile value (percent)	Percentile fire size		Percentage of historical fires larger than this size	Percentage of historical acres burned by fires larger than this size
	- ha -	- ac -		
99	1214	3000	1	69
98	554	1370	2	85
95	64	159	5	97
90	6	15	10	99

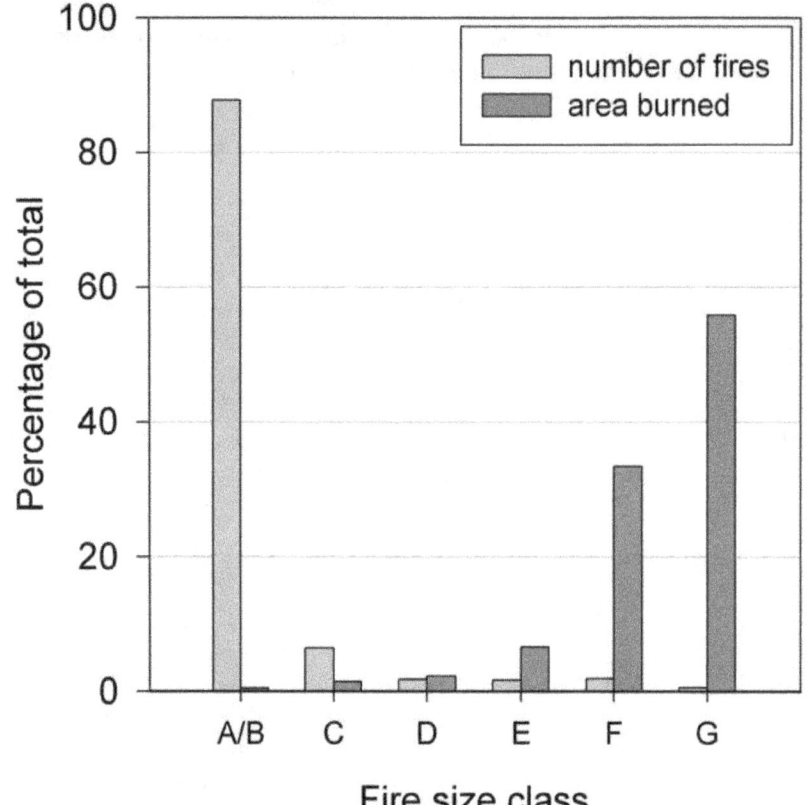

Figure 17—The historical relative distribution of the number of fires (left panel) and total acres burned (right panel) by fire size class. (A/B = fires less than 4 ha [10 ac]; C = 4 – 40 ha [10 – 100 ac]; D = 40 – 121 ha [100 - 300 ac]; E = 121 – 405 ha [300 – 1000 ac]; F = 405 – 2023 ha [1000 – 5000 ac]; G = more than 2023 ha [5000 ac]). The asymmetry between the number of fires and the area they burn suggests that smaller fires need not be considered when simulating burn probability because they contribute so little to it. Burn probability simulations typically focus on fires in size class D or E and larger.

USDA Forest Service Gen. Tech. Rep. RMRS-GTR-315. 2013

These charts illustrate the asymmetry between the number of wildfires and their contribution to acres burned. There are many more small fires than large fires, but they do not contribute much to the total area burned. From this chart we can tabulate the cumulative acres burned by wildfires of various percentile sizes (Table 15). The main purpose of this summary is to confirm that large fires do most of the "work" (burn acres), and to judge what size threshold may be most applicable on the landscape.

A third chart illustrates the seasonality of fire occurrence on a landscape by plotting the final fire size (common logarithm scale) against the date of fire start. If desired, the points can reflect different fire cause types, different regions of the landscape, or different vegetation types (Figure 18). This chart is useful for determining the earliest start dates of fires of different size classes, and for identifying differences in fire occurrence across a landscape. This is useful information when setting up a wildfire hazard simulation with FSim.

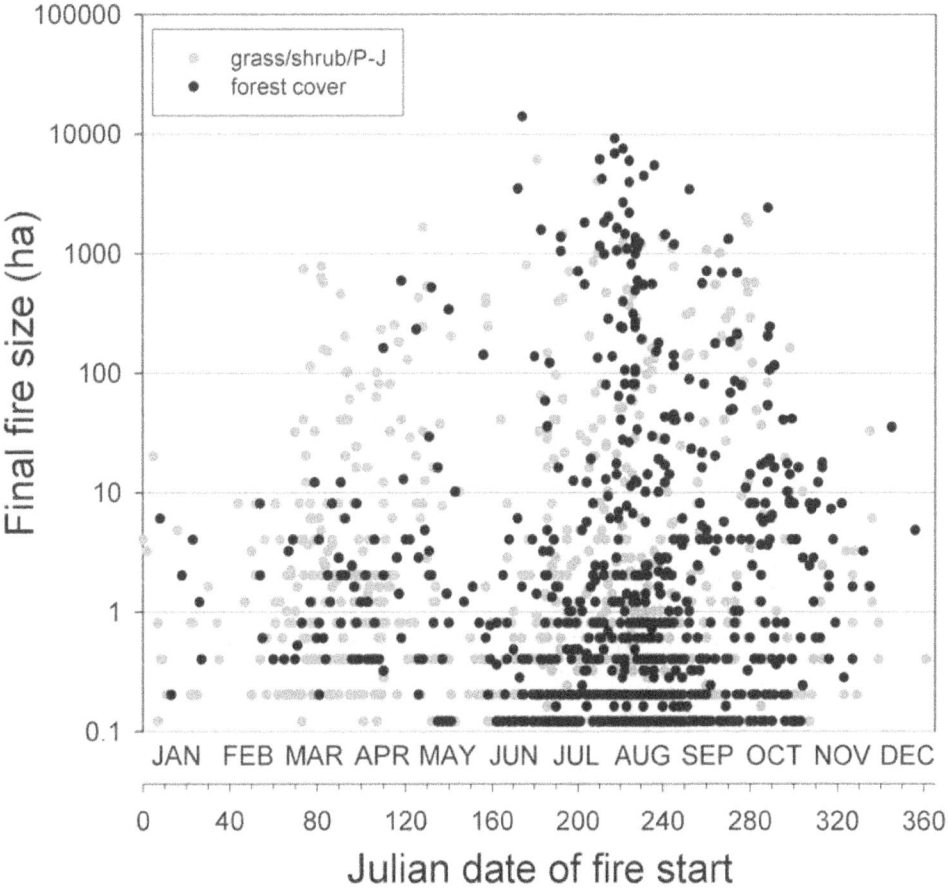

Figure 18—A chart showing the historical occurrence of wildfire in relation to their start date, final size and biophysical setting group on the Tetons Interagency Risk Assessment landscape. Wildfires occurring in the lower-elevation valley-bottoms dominated by sagebrush-grass and pinon-juniper vegetation types tend to start both earlier and later in the season, but do not account for as many acres burned as on areas dominated by timber-based fuel complexes.

The next step in the analysis of historical fire occurrence is the determination of co-efficients for a logistic regression of fire occurrence to *ERC-G* using FireFamily Plus. After the historical weather and historical occurrence data are imported into FireFamily Plus, a simple tool determines these coefficients for any specified threshold fire size. The threshold fire size is the minimum fire size to consider in the analysis; fires smaller than the threshold are excluded. The regression coefficients determine the daily probability that at least one wildfire larger than the threshold (P_{LFD}) will occur given the *ERC-G* value for the day. The form of the regression equation is:

$$P_{LFD} = \frac{1}{1 + e^{(-a+(-b*ERC))}} \qquad [5]$$

where *a* and *b* are coefficients determined for different minimum fire size thresholds (Table 16).

A separate analysis identifies the distribution of the daily number of fires exceeding the threshold given that at least one occurred. The mean of that distribution can be combined with the logistic regression model to determine the propensity for fires of different size classes to occur in relation to *ERC-G* (Table 16). The resulting probability of a large-fire day (LFD) as calculated from the regression is illustrated in Figure 19.

Table 16—Summary of coefficients for determining the probability of a large-fire day from a logistic regression equation for three large-fire size thresholds. More than one large fire can occur on a large-fire day, so the mean number of large fires per large-fire day is also indicated.

Threshold fire size		Regression coefficient		Mean number of fires per LFD
- ha -	- ac -	*a*	*b*	
4	10	-4.2217	0.0388	1.13
40	100	-5.1242	0.0444	1.14
121	300	-5.5398	0.0462	1.14

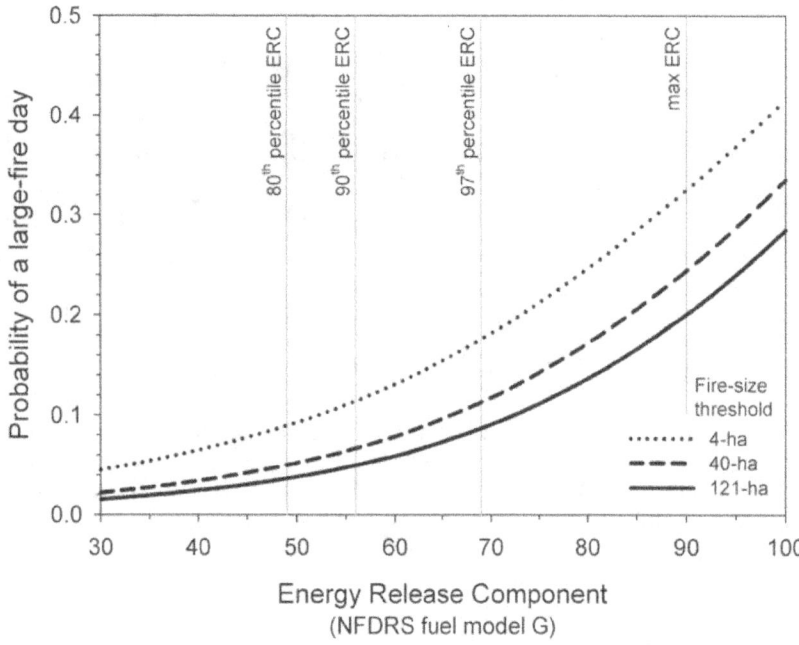

Figure 19—Results of the logistic regression daily fire occurrence probability coefficients determined for historical fires occurring in the Teton Interagency Risk Assessment landscape in relation to ERC-G measured at the Raspberry RAWS. This chart indicates the probability of at least one fire start that eventually exceeds the size thresholds. More than one large fire starts on many such large-fire days (see Table 16); this chart does not take into account the mean number of large fires per large-fire day.

USDA Forest Service Gen. Tech. Rep. RMRS-GTR-315. 2013

The final piece of fire occurrence information needed for a geospatial wildfire hazard assessment is a raster indicating the spatial likelihood of large-fire occurrence, based on the locations of historical wildfires on the landscape. For the TIARA, a logistic regression model was built to predict the spatial large-fire ignition likelihood (0 to 1) based on vegetation type, topographical variables, and distance to a road or trail (Scott and others 2012a). When large fires occur on this landscape, they tend to be located in the forested northwestern portion of the study area (Figure 20). The low-elevation grasslands do not produce many large fires, nor do the high-elevation areas of the major mountain ranges.

Near-Maximum Wildfire Behavior—A combination of fire behavior modeling and GIS software was used to simulate several measures of the near-maximum wildfire behavior (97th percentile wind speed and dead fuel moisture content). As described in Section 3, the 97th percentile probable maximum 1-minute average 6-m (20-ft) wind speed at the selected RAWS was 32 km/h (20 mi/hr); this wind speed value was applied in the upslope direction for all simulations of near-maximum wildfire behavior.

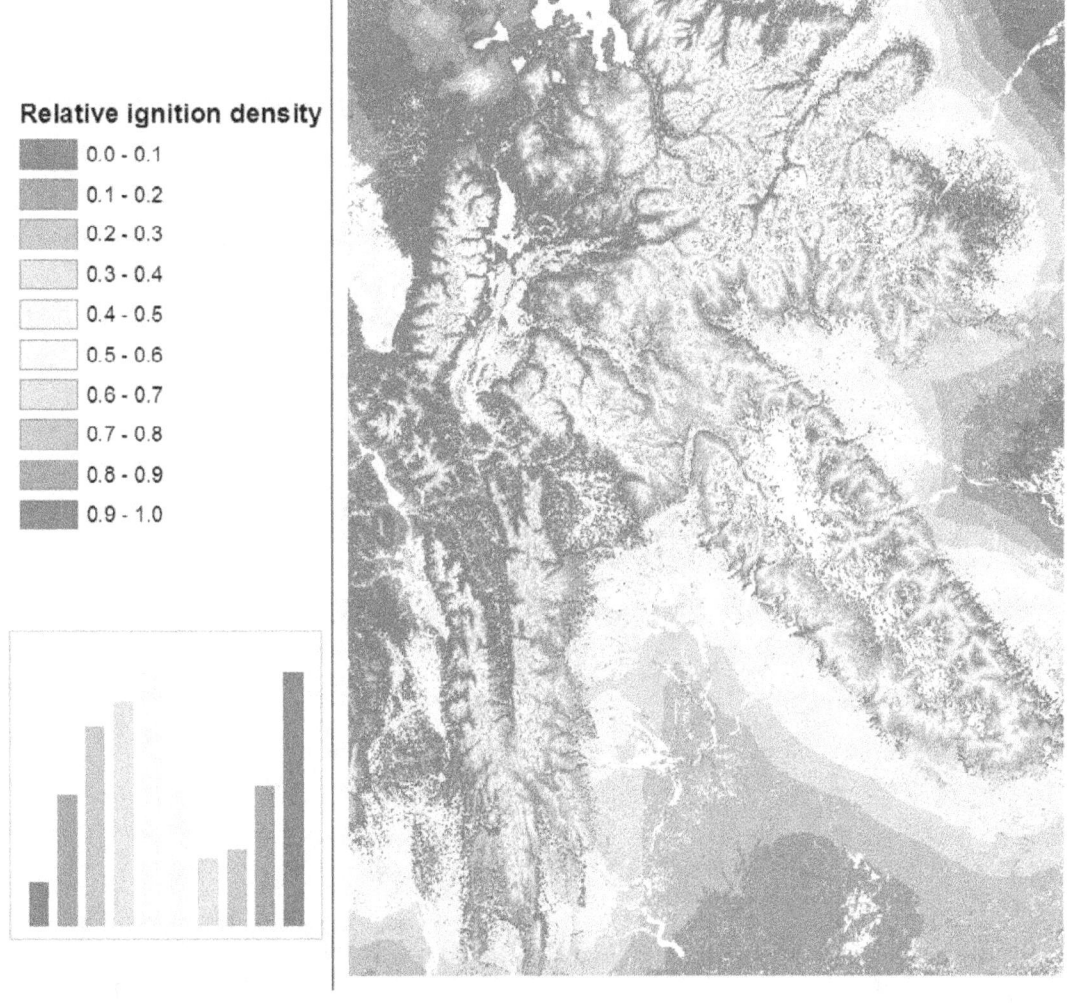

Relative ignition density

■	0.0 - 0.1
■	0.1 - 0.2
■	0.2 - 0.3
□	0.3 - 0.4
□	0.4 - 0.5
□	0.5 - 0.6
■	0.6 - 0.7
■	0.7 - 0.8
■	0.8 - 0.9
■	0.9 - 1.0

Figure 20—Relative large-fire ignition density across the Teton Interagency Risk Assessment landscape. Dark red areas have highest ignition density; dark blue have the lowest ignition density. White indicates zero ignition probability due to non-burnable fuel condition.

Also noted in Section 3, the 97th percentile 1-h timelag moisture content was determined from the FRISK file to be 3 percent, the 10-h timelag moisture content value was 4 percent, and the 100-h timelag moisture content was 8 percent. Live herbaceous fuel was assumed to be 45 percent, corresponding to fuel that is almost fully cured, and the live woody moisture content was assumed to be 75 percent. These moisture content values were applied to the entire landscape, regardless of aspect, elevation or canopy cover. FlamMap5 was used to simulate type of fire (with an adjustment for 'non-forest' fire), fireline intensity, and flame length for these weather conditions, with crown fire occurrence simulated with the 'Scott and Reinhardt 2001' option.

Non-forest fire dominates the landscape (Figure 21). More than half of the forested areas are simulated as passive crown fire for the near-maximum fire weather condition; only on a very small fraction is fully active crown fire possible. Passive crown fire encompasses a broad range of fire behavior, from single-tree torching to almost fully active crowning, so even passive crown fires can generate very high fireline intensity and flame length values. The majority of the area where passive crown fire is predicted would be likely to result in high-severity effects on the overstory vegetation. Non-burnable portions of the landscape include lakes, agricultural areas and bare ground at high elevation.

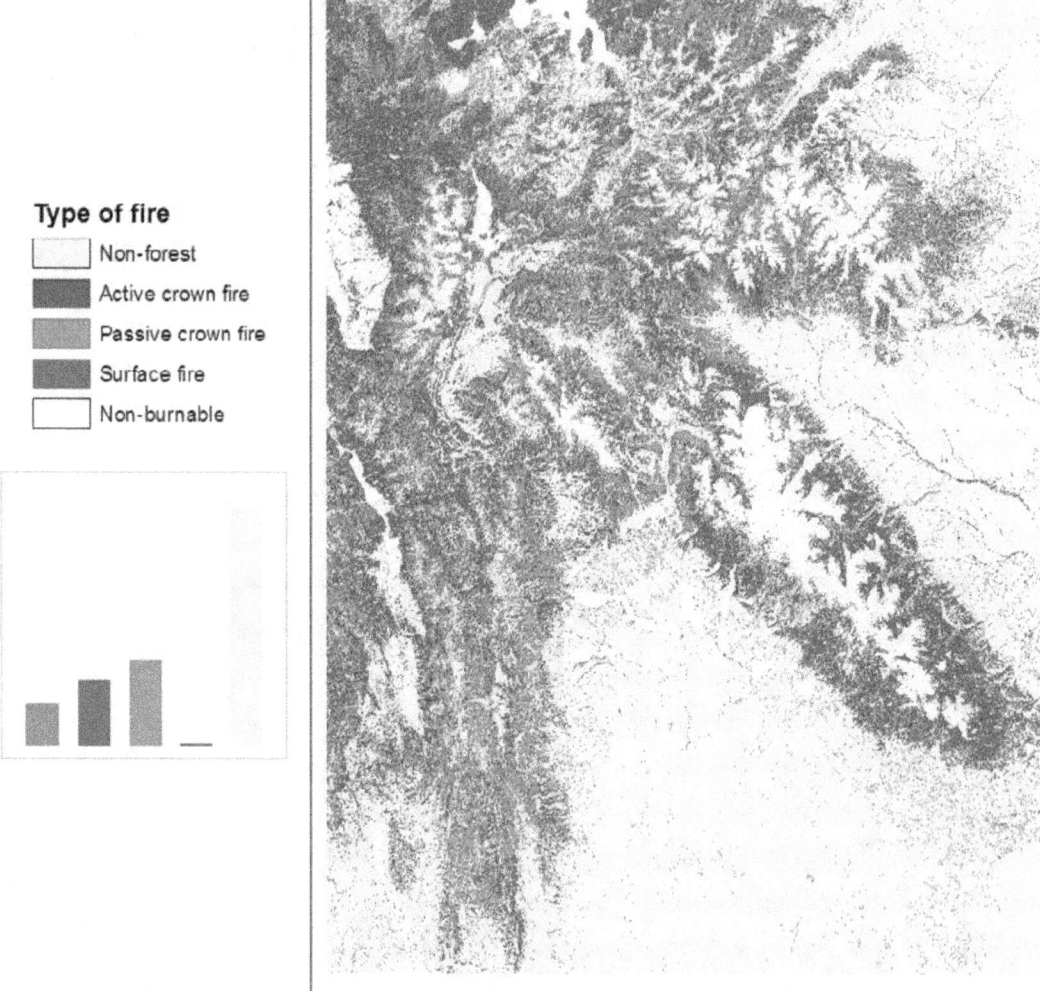

Figure 21—Type of fire classification for the near-maximum condition on the Teton Interagency Risk Assessment landscape. Non-forest fire dominates the landscape. Where conifer crown fires are possible, passive crown fire is most likely; only a small amount of active crown fire is possible. Inset histogram indicates the relative distribution of fire type across the entire landscape.

Near-maximum fireline intensity spans the entire spectrum from class I where spread is slow in light fuel to class V where active crown fire and high-grade passive crown fire is simulated (Figure 22). The modal intensity class is IV-, corresponding to the large, non-forest areas of the landscape mapped to fuel models GS2 and GR2.

Near-maximum flame length (Figure 23) exhibits a pattern similar to that of fireline intensity. A small portion of the landscape is mapped as capable of producing flame lengths in excess of 50 feet. The 8–12 foot flame-length class is the most prevalent, again corresponding primarily to the non-forest portions of the landscape mapped to GS2 and GR2.

Wildfire Likelihood—FSim was used to estimate annual *BP* across the TIARA landscape. The bulk of the area is in the two classes representing a *BP* of 0.001 to 0.004 (Figure 24). These high-likelihood areas of the landscape correspond to land covered by grass and grass-shrub surface fuel, which exhibit high spread rates. The low-likelihood areas of the landscape correspond to areas with low spread rates, large non-burnable areas, and low historical ignition probability (see Figure 20).

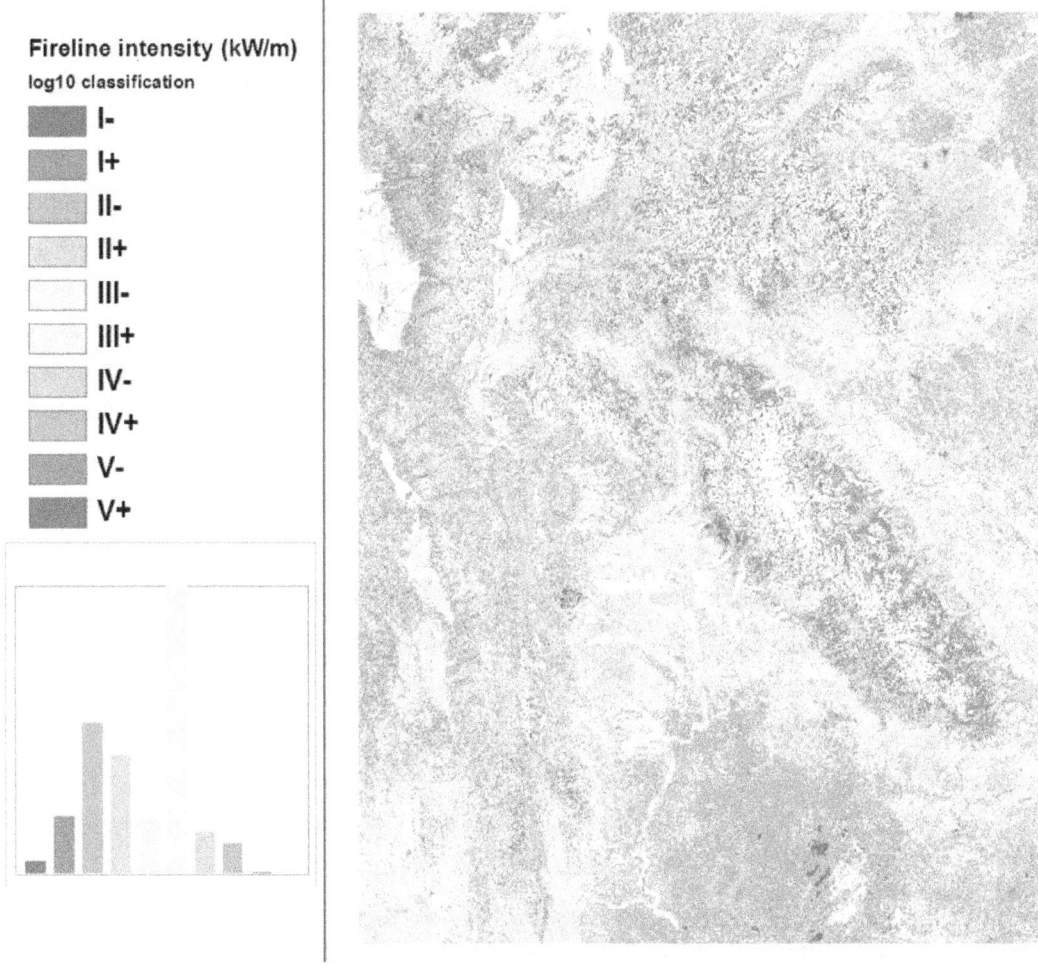

Figure 22—Near-maximum fireline intensity (kW/m) for the Teton Interagency Risk Assessment landscape, displayed on a logarithmic scale. The inset histogram indicates a preponderance of the class IV- (Table 4), corresponding to the large area of grass-shrub fuel type surrounding the south and east flanks of the mountain ranges.

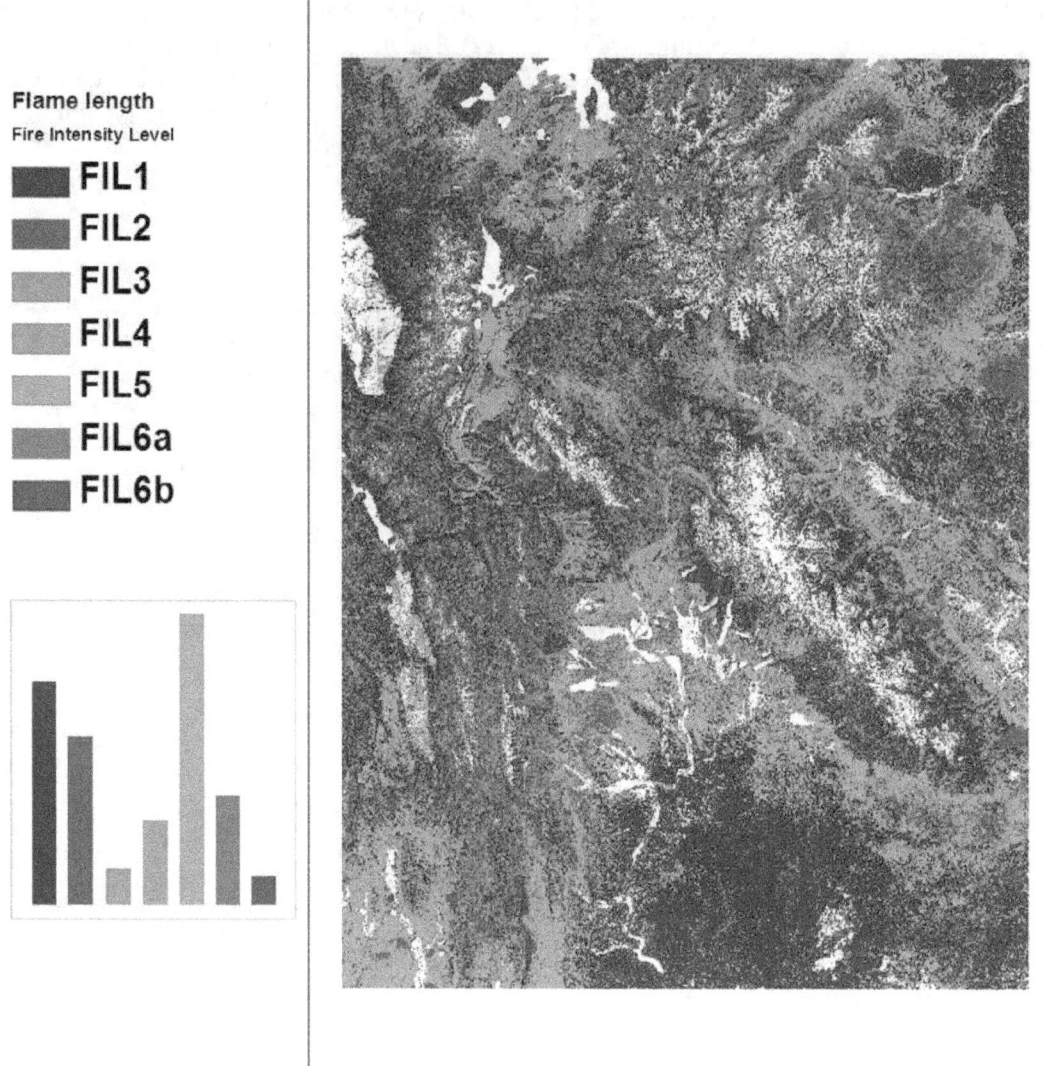

Figure 2—Near-maximum flame length for the Teton Interagency Landscape. Flame length classes are the six standard Fire Intensity Levels, plus an additional class break at 15 m (50 ft). The inset histogram indicates a preponderance of area in the 2.4 – 3.7 m (8-12 ft) flame-length class, corresponding to the large area of grass-shrub fuel type surrounding the south and east flanks of the mountain ranges.

52

USDA Forest Service Gen. Tech. Rep. RMRS-GTR-315. 2013

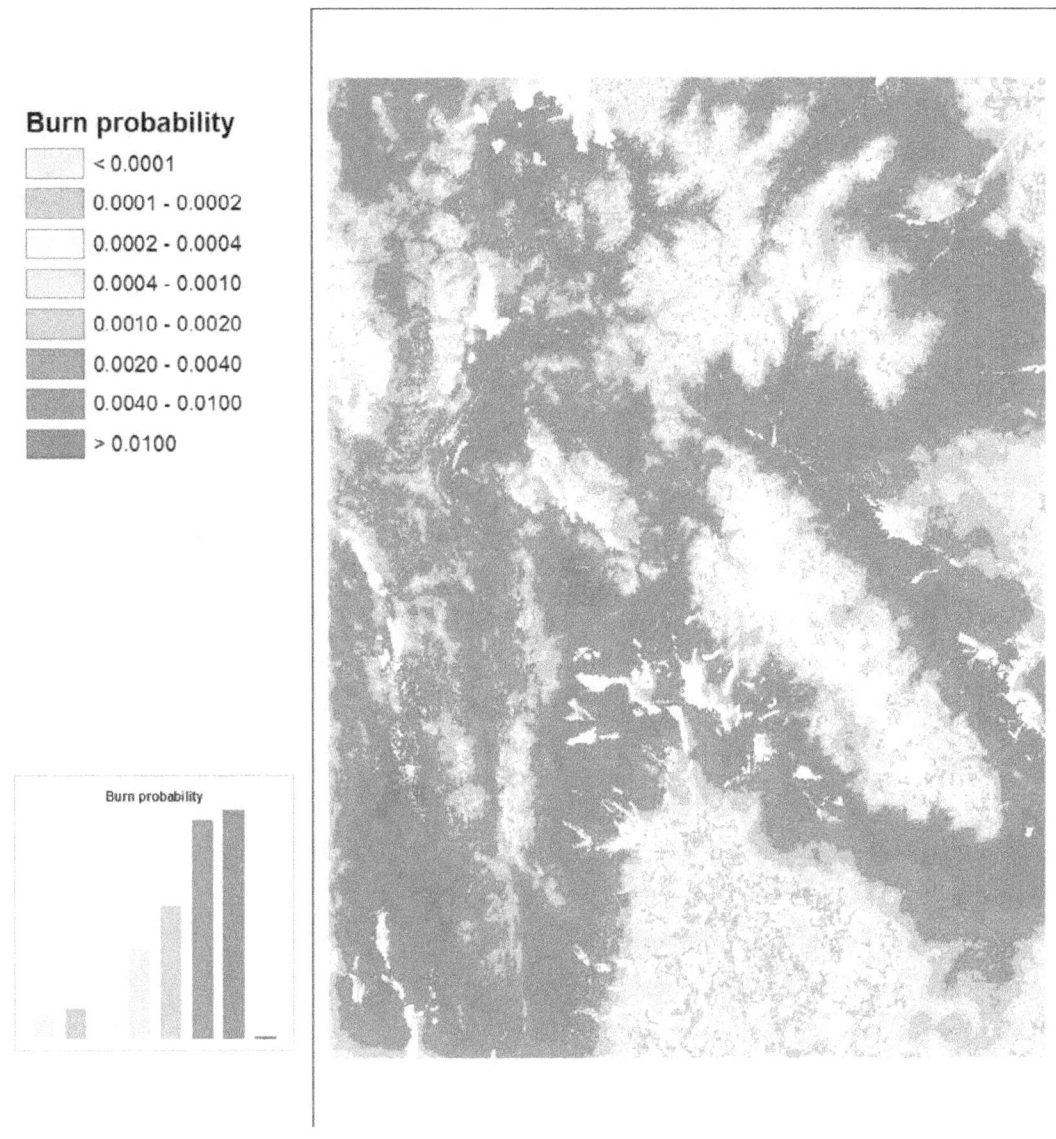

Burn probability

	< 0.0001
	0.0001 - 0.0002
	0.0002 - 0.0004
	0.0004 - 0.0010
	0.0010 - 0.0020
	0.0020 - 0.0040
	0.0040 - 0.0100
	> 0.0100

Figure 24—Annual burn probability across the Teton Interagency Risk Assessment landscape. Non-burnable areas, consisting mainly of bare ground at high-elevation and lakes, are shown in white. The inset histogram illustrates the distribution of likelihood across the classes.

Conditional Wildfire Intensity—FSim was also used to estimate two measures of conditional wildfire intensity: mean fireline intensity (MFI) and conditional flame length (*CFL*). *MFI* is a direct output of FSim; *CFL* is calculated as the expected value of flame length based on flame length probabilities. Both measures incorporate the effects of variability in fuel moisture, wind speed and wind direction, as well as the effects of spread direction. Unlike measures of potential fire intensity, conditional wildfire intensity does not assume a headfire, but instead uses simulation modeling that implicitly incorporates the effect of non-heading spread on wildfire intensity. For these reasons, *MFI* (Figure 25) is typically lower than the near-maximum fire intensity (Figure 22), and *CFL* (Figure 26) is lower than near-maximum flame length (Figure 23).

USDA Forest Service Gen. Tech. Rep. RMRS-GTR-315. 2013

53

Mean fireline intensity

log10 classification

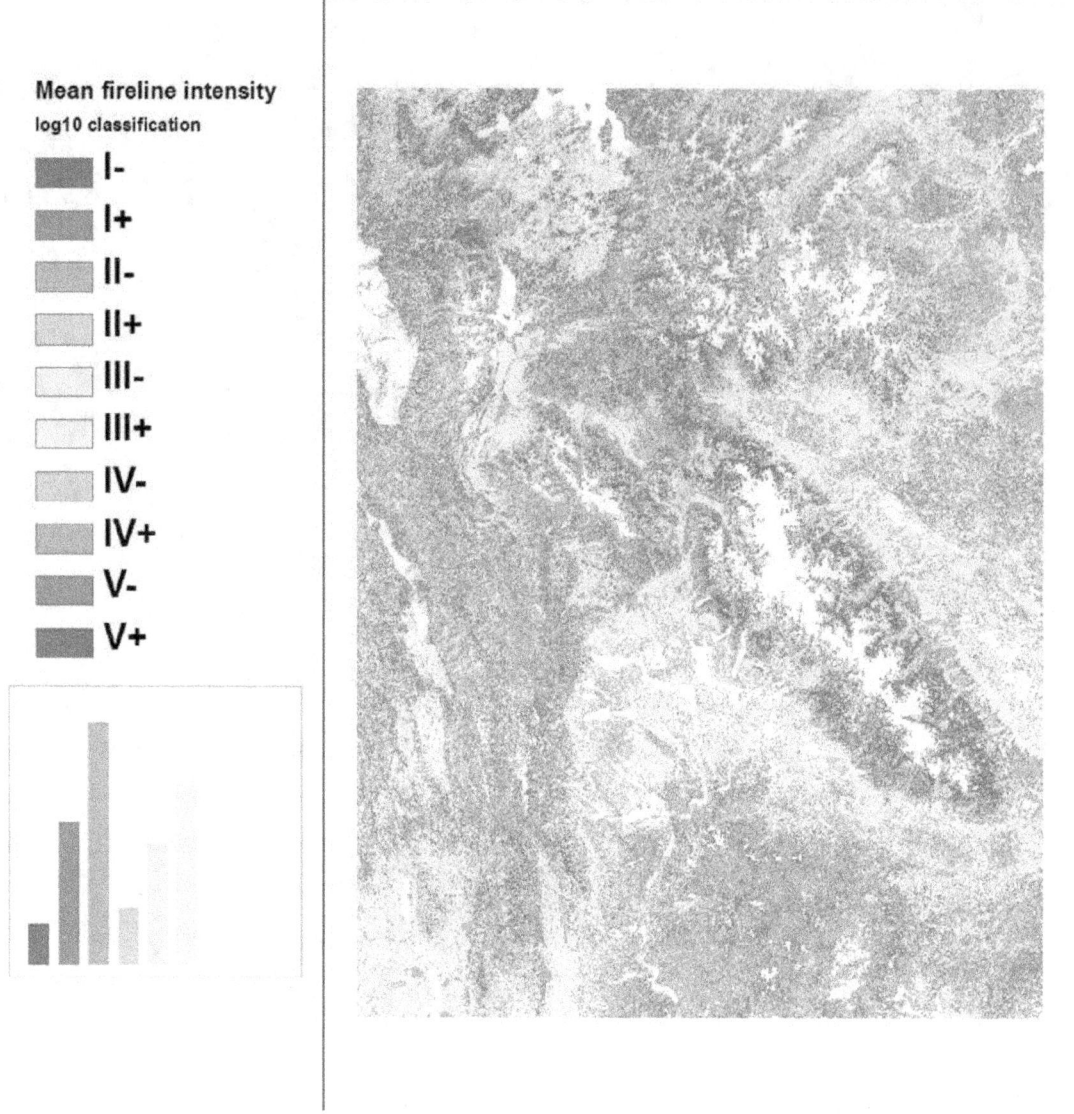

I-
I+
II-
II+
III-
III+
IV-
IV+
V-
V+

Figure 2—Mean fireline intensity (scaled by its common logarithm) across the Teton Interagency Risk Assessment landscape.

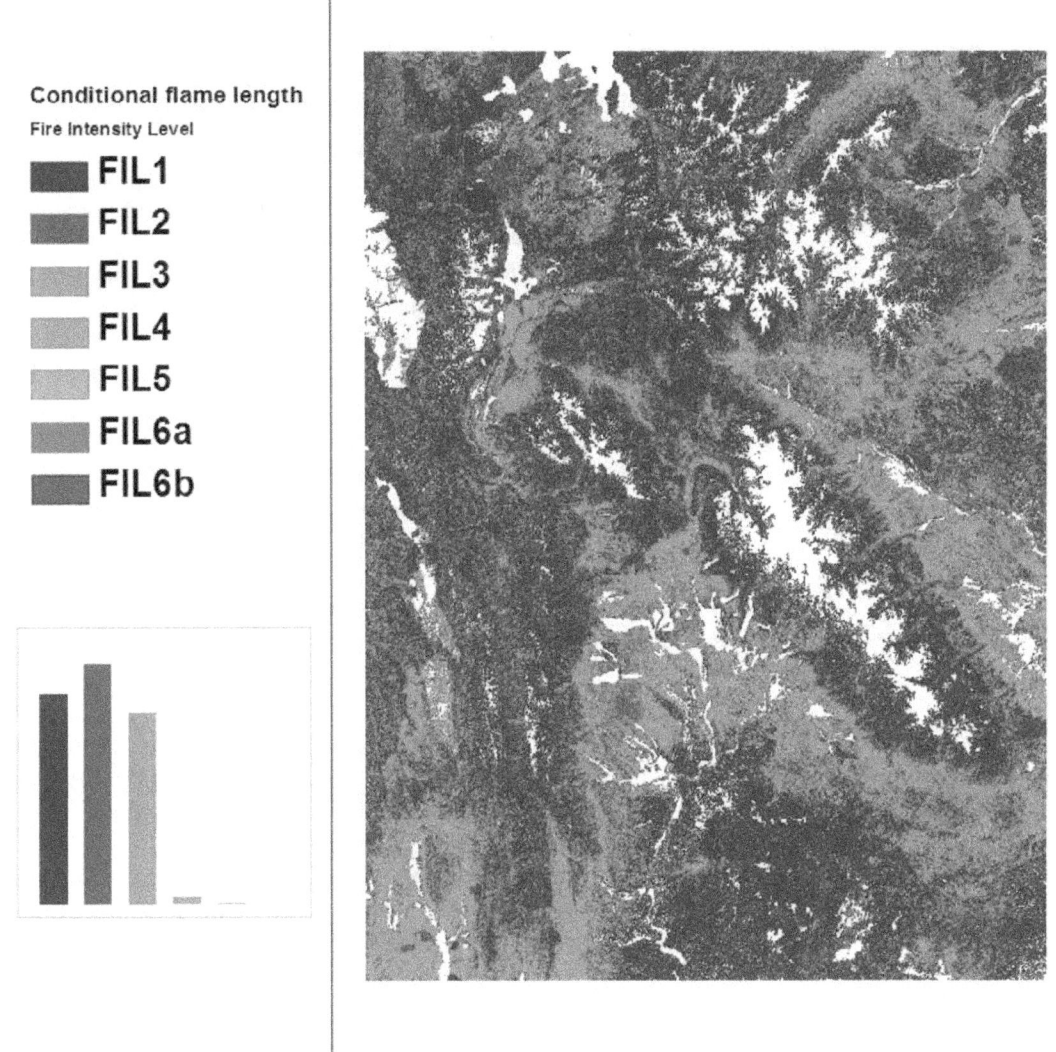

Conditional flame length

Fire Intensity Level

- FIL1
- FIL2
- FIL3
- FIL4
- FIL5
- FIL6a
- FIL6b

Figure 2—Conditional flame length (CFL) across the Teton Interagency Risk Assessment landscape. CFL is an estimate of the characteristic flame length at each pixel, given the fuel characteristics at the pixel in conjunction with the distribution of fire weather. CFL includes the effect of relative spread direction (heading, flanking, backing, etc.) on flame length.

USDA Forest Service Gen. Tech. Rep. RMRS-GTR-315. 2013

55

HVRA Characterization

HVRA Identification—Initially, BTNF fire managers and resource specialists, joined by Wyoming Game and Fish biologists, gathered together to create an initial list of possible HVRAs. Forest Leadership identified certain resources and assets as 'highly valued' based on their importance in driving fire management decision making. For example, infrastructure was identified as an HVRA because depicting the potential for loss to infrastructure helps identify considerations for managing a natural ignition. Similarly, aspen stands (specifically those determined to be a high priority for restoration) were also identified as a highly valued resource. Capturing the potential for wildfire benefit to these stands may help identify prescribed fire treatments or craft objectives for managing a wildfire. Recognizing the basic land management direction to steward the fire-adapted ecosystems present on their landscapes and the desire to have vegetation in its historical mix of structure and composition, the BTNF staff determined that they needed an HVRA that would characterize the 'diverse and resilient vegetation' of fire-adapted ecosystems.

The list of individual HVRAs identified for an analysis area can be quite long, suggesting a two-level hierarchical structure to organize HVRAs (Thompson and others 2013a). The primary HVRA represents a group of similar HVRAs. The individual HVRAs within a primary HVRA are called sub-HVRAs. HVRAs and sub-HVRAs can be assigned different response functions and different relative importance values. In some cases, an additional variable—called a covariate—may have been identified by resource specialists as an important HVRA characteristic affecting the HVRA's response to wildfire. A covariate (soil erosion class, for example) results in a different response function, but the relative importance is the same as the HVRA or sub-HVRA to which it belongs. On the BTNF, the Forest ultimately identified seven primary HVRAs to be analyzed in this assessment (Table 17).

The Investments HVRA represents infrastructure within and adjacent to the BTNF. This HVRA includes investments made by the Forest Service as well as those made by cooperating agencies and holders of special use permits. The Investments HVRA consists of nine sub-HVRAs mapped on and within 1 mile of the Forest boundary. Data on the Wyoming Game and Fish elk feed grounds were provided by the Wyoming Game and Fish Department. Oil and gas development area data were provided by the Wyoming Oil and Gas Commission. Power line data were provided by Lower Valley Energy. Remaining sub-HVRA data were derived from the Forest's corporate geospatial data set.

The wildland urban interface HVRA represents areas on the Forest closest to private land. The HVRA has two sub-HVRAs: the WUI defense zone and the portion of the Protection Fire Management Unit (FMU) outside the WUI defense zone. The WUI defense zone is characterized as NFS land within a 0.25 mile buffer of private land. This sub-HVRA represents the area of highest interest for fuel reduction projects. The Protection FMU outside the WUI defense zone captures the balance of the Forest lands that predominantly receive a suppression response to wildfires due to their proximity to values at risk. The Protection FMU is characterized in the Forest's Fire Management Plan (USDA Forest Service 2012). The sub-HVRAs were derived from the Forest's corporate geospatial dataset.

The critical fish and wildlife habitat HVRA represents habitat components of four wildlife and three fish species. Sage-grouse is a candidate species for listing as endangered. Pronghorn antelope, bighorn sheep, and moose are all species whose habitat needs are of concern to the Wyoming Game and Fish Department. The fish species—Northern leatherside chub, and Bonneville and Colorado River cutthroat trout—are

Table 17—Highly valued resources and assets (HVRAs) and sub-HVRAs identified in the BTNF risk assessment.

Primary HVRA	Sub-HVRAs
Investments	Feed grounds
	Special use permit areas
	Trailheads/boating sites
	Campgrounds/picnic areas
	Cabins/guard stations/lookouts
	Oil and gas development areas
	Communication sites
	Power lines
	White bark pine plus trees
WUI	WUI defense zone
	Protection FMU
Critical fish and wildlife habitat	Pronghorn migration routes
	Bighorn migration routes
	Moose thermal cover
	Sage grouse core areas
	Sage grouse near leks
	Trout and chub streams
Priority vegetation	Whitebark pine A
	Whitebark pine B
	Whitebark pine C
	Whitebark pine D
	Sensitive plants
	Feedground Aspen
	Aspen (high priority)
Watershed	Municipal watershed (DFC4)
Diverse and resilient vegetation	Subalpine dry-mesic spruce-fir
	Montane sagebrush steppe
	Subalpine parkland
	Subalpine wet-mesic spruce-fir
	Aspen forest and woodland
	Montane Douglas-fir
Timber base	Desired Future Condition 1B
	Desired Future Condition 10

proposed candidates for listing. This sub-HVRA was mapped as 6th level Hydrologic Unit Code (HUC) watershed boundaries occupied by those species. The 6th level HUC was used because only fire over the entire watershed would impact the fishes' habitat. Pronghorn antelope migration routes are split into conifer and non-conifer covariates. Geospatial data for all sub-HVRAs, with the exception of fisheries, were obtained from the Wyoming Game and Fish Department. The fisheries sub-HVRA was derived from existing USFS data.

USDA Forest Service Gen. Tech. Rep. RMRS-GTR-315. 2013

57

The priority vegetation HVRA represents Threatened, Endangered, Sensitive, and Proposed Candidate vegetation on the Forest that is sensitive to wildfire (positive or negative). The priority vegetation HVRA also represents aspen stands that are particularly sensitive to wildfire (positive or negative). Aspen was identified as a species of particular interest given its decline throughout the region and its critical role as wildlife habitat. The HVRA is split into seven sub-HVRAs. Whitebark pine data were obtained from the Greater Yellowstone Coordinating Committee (GYCC) Whitebark sub-committee. The whitebark pine stands were then split into four sub-HVRAs (A-D) based on the extent of canopy damage and anticipated fire effects. This characterization was provided by the GYCC Whitebark sub-committee co-chair. The sensitive plants sub-HVRA is further split into two covariates representing those species that have a positive response to fire and those that have a negative response. Data for these plants were provided by the BTNF botanist, based on the Wyoming Natural Diversity Database. Aspen adjacent to elk feed grounds may be damaged post-fire due to intensive herbivory by elk. These aspen stands at risk were identified by the Wyoming Game and Fish department, based on the Forest's 2007 vegetation map (USDA Forest Service 2007). The high restoration priority aspen is based on the Campbell and Bartos (2001) aspen risk key used in the Grey's River Aspen Assessment (Loosen and others 2009). These high restoration priority aspen stands are limited to those identified during the Greys River Aspen Assessment.

The municipal watersheds HVRA represents areas identified by the Desired Future Condition (DFC) of the same name in the Forest Plan (USDA Forest Service 1990). Data for the municipal watersheds HVRA were obtained from the Forest's corporate geospatial dataset.

The diverse and resilient vegetation HVRA (DRV) represents the combination of vegetation communities and their distribution of successional states. This study assumes that the reference condition distribution of successional states present in fire-adapted vegetation communities equates to diverse and resilient vegetation communities. The Forest wanted to capture diverse and resilient vegetation as an HVRA in order to capture both its importance as the cornerstone of successful land management and as a proxy for fire's role in fire-adapted ecosystems. Six sub-HVRAs are characterized as the bio-physical settings shown in Table 17. Each sub-HVRA was further split into covariates that represent whether the current percentage of the individual succession classes are in deficit, similar, or in surplus when compared to the mean percentage under the historical range of variation. Reference conditions were acquired from LANDFIRE vegetation dynamics models. The sub-HVRAs and covariates were derived from LANDFIRE geospatial data using the Fire Regime Condition Class mapping tool (Helmbrecht and others 2013).

The timber base HVRA represents two DFC areas identified in the 1990 Forest Plan (USDA Forest Service 1990) where commercial timber harvest activities may take place. DFC 1B refers to areas of substantial commodity resource development and DFC 10 refers to areas of simultaneous development of resources and other opportunities. The sub-HVRAs were derived from the Forest's corporate geospatial dataset.

Response to Wildfire—The analysis quantifies wildfire response as the expected value of net response (Finney 2005). This approach has previously been applied to national, regional, and forest-level assessments of wildfire response (Scott and Helmbrecht 2010; Thompson and others 2011; Helmbrecht and others 2012; Thompson and others 2013a, b). The analysis relies on local resource specialists to produce a tabular response function for each HVRA occurring in the analysis area. A response function is a tabulation of the relative change in value of an HVRA if it were to burn in each of six fire intensity levels (FILs), represented as flame length classes (Table 5). A positive value in a response function indicates a benefit, or increase in value; a negative value indicates a loss, or decrease in value. Response function values ranged from -100 (greatest possible loss of resource value) to +100 (greatest increase in value). Covariates are other environmental variables (with supporting geospatial data) that could affect HVRA response to fire. Response functions for the BTNF HVRAs (Table 18) were generated during a 2-day workshop. Resource and fire management specialists were present and participated in assigning the response functions.

Relative Importance—In order to integrate HVRAs with differing units of measure (for example, habitat vs. timber), relative importance (*RI*) values were assigned to each HVRA by Forest line officers. Relative importance values were developed by first ranking the HVRAs, then assigning an *RI* value to each. The most important HVRA was assigned *RI* = 100. Each remaining HVRA was then assigned an *RI* value indicating its importance relative to that most-important HVRA.

The *RI* values apply to the overall HVRA on the Forest as a whole, not a unit area of HVRA. The calculations need to take into account the relative extent of each HVRA to avoid overemphasizing HVRAs that cover many acres. This was accomplished by normalizing the calculations by the relative extent (*RE*) of each HVRA on the forest. Relative extent refers to the number of pixels mapped to each HVRA. In using this method, the relative importance of each HVRA is spread out over the HVRA's extent. An HVRA with few pixels can have a high importance per pixel; an HVRA with a great many pixels has a low importance per pixel.

Each HVRA and sub-HVRA was assigned a value of Relative Importance in order to permit weighting the HVRAs together. On the BTNF, the WUI and Investments HVRAs were assigned a relative importance of 100, the highest possible value (Table 19). Habitat, Priority Vegetation, and Municipal Watersheds were assigned 70 to 75 percent of the maximum importance. Diverse and Resilient Vegetation (DRV) was given 50 percent, and the timber resource just 15 percent of maximum importance. These *RI* values are divided by the extent of each HVRA, in terms of the number of pixels, to produce the final weighting factor for each HVRA—relative importance per unit relative extent.

Table 18—Response functions for selected HVRAs on the Bridger-Teton National Forest HVRAs. Please see Scott and others (2013) for a complete listing of response function values for the Critical Fish and Wildlife Habitat, Diverse Resilient Vegetation, and Priority Vegetation HVRAs.

HVRA Name	Sub-HVRA Name	FIL 1	FIL 2	FIL 3	FIL 4	FIL 5	FIL 6
Investments	Game and Fish feedgrounds	-50	-70	-90	-100	-100	-100
	Special use permit areas	-50	-70	-90	-100	-100	-100
	Trailheads/boating sites	0	-10	-20	-30	-40	-50
	Campgrounds/picnic areas	0	-10	-20	-55	-75	-75
	Cabins/guard stations	-50	-70	-90	-100	-100	-100
	Oil and gas development	-10	-20	-40	-80	-100	-100
	Communication sites	0	-30	-60	-80	-100	-100
	Power lines	-10	-20	-40	-80	-100	-100
	Whitebark pine plus trees	-10	-70	-100	-100	-100	-100
Wildland urban Interface	WUI defense zone	0	-50	-75	-100	-100	-100
	Protection FMU	10	0	-25	-50	-50	-50
Watershed	Municipal Watershed (DFC 4)	20	0	-20	-50	-75	-100
Timber base	Desired future condition 1B	20	-20	-50	-80	-100	-100
	Desired future condition 10	50	25	10	0	-25	-50

Table 19—Relative importance (RI), relative extent (RE) and relative importance per unit relative extent (RI/RE) for primary and sub-HVRAs on the Bridger-Teton National Forest. RI/RE are expressed on a logarithmic scale; smallest RI/RE = 1.0.

Primary HVRA	RI	Sub-HVRAs	RI	RE (ha)	RI/RE $\log_{10}$
Investments	100	Feed grounds	8.1	6	6.3
		Special use permit areas	13.5	3,152	3.7
		Trailheads/boating sites	4.7	34	5.2
		Campgrounds/picnic areas	11.5	175	4.9
		Cabins/guard stations/lookouts	13.5	9	6.3
		Oil and gas development areas	13.5	5,251	3.5
		Communication sites	13.5	2	7.0
		Power lines	13.5	4,081	3.6
		White bark pine plus trees	8.1	4	6.4
WUI	100	WUI defense zone	58.8	52,223	3.1
		Protection FMU	41.2	79,963	2.8
Critical fish and wildlife habitat	75	Pronghorn migration routes	5.1	17,655	2.5
		Bighorn migration routes	10.2	22,680	2.7
		Moose thermal cover	11.9	14,951	3.0
		Sage grouse core areas	17	2,203	4.0
		Sage grouse near leks	13.6	8,028	3.3
		Trout and chub streams	8.5	476,520	1.3
Priority vegetation	75	Whitebark pine A	22.6	57,244	2.7
		Whitebark pine B	4.5	80,100	1.8
		Whitebark pine C	18.1	62,013	2.6
		Whitebark pine D	0.0	4,967	--
		Sensitive plants	6.8	131,690	1.8
		Feedground Aspen	3.8	3,487	3.1
		Aspen (high priority)	19.2	11,518	3.3
Watershed	70	Municipal watershed (DFC4)	70.0	22,200	3.6
Diverse and resilient vegetation	50	Subalpine dry-mesic spruce-fir	4.1	511,033	1.0
		Montane sagebrush steppe	13.5	146,293	2.1
		Subalpine parkland	9.5	156,142	1.9
		Subalpine wet-mesic spruce-fir	2.7	128,038	1.4
		Aspen forest and woodland	13.5	132,215	2.1
		Montane Douglas-fir	6.8	70,279	2.1
Timber base	15	Desired Future Condition 1B	8.8	73,991	2.2
		Desired Future Condition 10	6.2	311,849	1.4

Exposure Analysis

The exposure of HVRAs to wildfire on the BTNF was accomplished by characterizing, where each HVRA occurs, the near-maximum fire intensity and type of fire, annual burn probability, and conditional fire intensity. Detailed results for the WUI HVRAs (both the defense and protection zones) are shown in Figure 27. Each small black dot represents the combination of *BP* and near-maximum *FLI* at a single pixel; a systematic sample (0.1 percent, or 1 out of 1000) of the total number of WUI pixels is shown. The large gray dots represent the average BP and *FLI* in each zone. The distribution of *BP* and *FLI* are similar in the two zones; on average, the protection zone is exposed to slightly

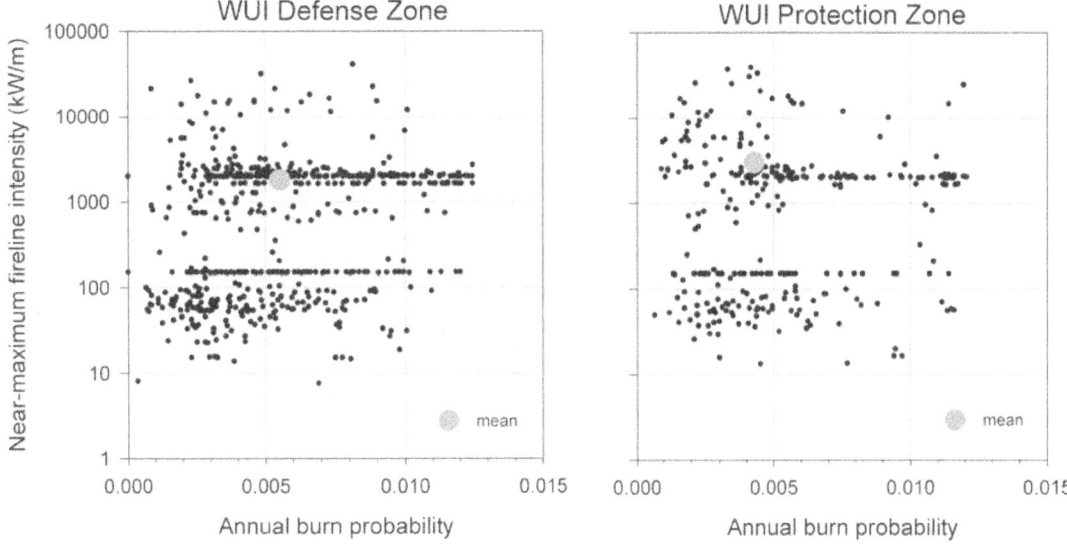

Figure 2—Exposure of Wildland Urban Interface (WUI) defense zone and protection zone to wildfire on the Bridger-Teton National Forest. The gray dot on each panel shows the mean burn probability and mean fireline intensity. Y-axis is the near-maximum fireline intensity (97th percentile condition).

higher near-maximum *FLI* values (Table 20) and slightly lower BP values (Table 21) than the defense zone. Although the near-maximum *FLI* is greater in the protection zone, the conditional mean *FLI* is greater in the defense zone (Table 21), indicating a difference in fuel structure between these two zones.

The mean exposure of each HVRA to wildfire is depicted in Figure 28 and Figure 29. Focusing on the Investments HVRA, the Wyoming Fish and Game feedgrounds are exposed to the highest *BP* and *FLI*, whereas the communication sites are exposed to the lowest *BP* and *FLI* values.

These results address only the likelihood of experiencing a fire and the conditional mean or near-maximum fire intensity and type of fire. They do not consider the effect of various intensity levels on the HVRA, nor do they incorporate the importance of the different HVRAs relative to one another. Those results are addressed in the next section.

Effects Analysis

Effects analysis results are integrated across all HVRAs and described for the whole BTNF using the weighted sum described in Equation 2. All HVRAs were clipped to the Forest boundary except investments, which were clipped to 1 mile of the Forest boundary. Results for the investments HVRA that occur outside the Forest boundary are labeled "non-Forest" in the ranger district summary below.

The most general indicator of potential for wildfire effects at a grid cell is the number of overlapping HVRAs at that cell—the more overlapping HVRAs present, the greater the potential for effects. Because this assessment includes the DRV HVRA, which covers nearly all of the landscape, only 8 percent of the landscape is not covered by any HVRA (Figure 30). Sixty-five percent of the landscape is covered by just one or two HVRAs, whereas four or more HVRAs overlap on seven percent of the landscape. Because the wildfire risk measure, E(*wNVC*), sums the risk associated with overlapping HVRAs, the effects of multiple HVRAs can be additive, if their effects are uniformly positive or negative, or offsetting, if some HVRAs exhibit a positive E(*NVC*) whereas others are negative.

Table 20—Exposure of highly valued resources and assets to wildfire on the Bridger-Teton National Forest based on near-maximum potential wildfire behavior.

Primary HVRA	Sub-HVRA	Type of fire[a]					Mean intensity	
		NB	NF	S	P	A	FLI	FL
		Percentage of sub-HVRA					kW/m	m
Investments	Feed grounds	0	71	0	29	0	4,777	5.2
	Special use permit areas	6	34	31	28	2	2,387	3.1
	Trailheads/boating sites	5	62	17	17	0	1,005	1.8
	Campgrounds/picnic areas	5	38	26	29	1	1,991	2.6
	Cabins/guard stations/lookouts	0	73	9	18	0	1,726	2.6
	Oil and gas development areas	0	47	19	30	3	3,310	4.1
	Communication sites	50	50	0	0	0	75	0.4
	Power lines	12	63	17	8	0	1,272	1.9
	White bark pine plus trees	0	20	20	60	0	925	2.0
WUI	WUI defense zone	2	59	23	15	0	1,796	2.5
	Protection FMU	3	38	29	28	2	3,005	3.7
Critical fish and wildlife habitat	Pronghorn migration routes	4	68	13	16	0	1,817	2.6
	Bighorn migration routes	25	37	16	21	1	1,775	2.4
	Moose thermal cover	0	0	28	71	1	5,346	6.9
	Sage grouse core areas	10	66	16	7	0	1,460	2.0
	Sage grouse near leks	0	93	4	3	0	1,512	2.1
	Trout and chub streams	11	33	22	33	1	2,308	3.1
Priority vegetation	Whitebark pine A	7	18	35	39	1	1,609	2.4
	Whitebark pine B	5	12	37	45	1	1,705	2.6
	Whitebark pine C	5	16	37	42	1	1,771	2.6
	Whitebark pine D	4	31	29	36	0	871	1.7
	Sensitive plants	10	36	24	30	1	1,789	2.6
	Feedground Aspen	0	55	28	17	0	2,005	2.7
	Aspen (high priority)	0	20	39	39	2	3,718	4.5
Watershed	Municipal watershed (DFC4)	13	27	23	23	3	3,750	4.4
Diverse and resilient vegetation	Subalpine dry-mesic spruce-fir	1	18	23	56	2	3,523	4.7
	Montane sagebrush steppe	0	100	0	0	0	1,503	2.0
	Subalpine parkland	5	27	29	38	1	1,255	2.0
	Subalpine wet-mesic spruce-fir	0	14	15	69	2	5,467	6.9
	Aspen forest and woodland	0	12	73	15	0	1,019	1.7
	Montane Douglas-fir	0	13	61	24	2	2,825	3.4
Timber base	Desired Future Condition 1B	0	30	19	50	1	3,356	4.6
	Desired Future Condition 10	1	36	24	39	1	3,120	4.1

[a] NB = non-burnable; NF = non-forest; S = surface; P = passive crown; A = active crown

Table 21—Exposure of highly valued resources and assets to wildfire on the Bridger-Teton National Forest based on results from FSim.

Primary	Sub-HVRA	Burn probability	Mean fireline intensity	Conditional flame length
		fraction	kW/m	m
Investments	Feed grounds	0.00565	873	1.2
	Special use permit areas	0.00284	297	0.8
	Trailheads/boating sites	0.00243	326	0.8
	Campgrounds/picnic areas	0.00315	350	0.9
	Cabins/guard stations/lookouts	0.00380	354	0.9
	Oil and gas development areas	0.00253	367	0.9
	Communication sites	0.00148	37	0.2
	Power lines	0.00433	539	1.0
	White bark pine plus trees	0.00300	165	0.8
WUI	WUI defense zone	0.00553	543	1.1
	Protection FMU	0.00428	391	0.9
Critical fish and wildlife habitat	Pronghorn migration routes	0.00592	592	1.1
	Bighorn migration routes	0.00241	238	0.6
	Moose thermal cover	0.00169	119	0.6
	Sage grouse core areas	0.00556	639	1.1
	Sage grouse near leks	0.00754	794	1.3
	Trout and chub streams	0.00217	238	0.7
Priority vegetation	Whitebark pine A	0.00124	158	0.6
	Whitebark pine B	0.00111	138	0.6
	Whitebark pine C	0.00130	141	0.6
	Whitebark pine D	0.00212	270	0.8
	Sensitive plants	0.00225	237	0.7
	Feedground Aspen	0.00637	492	1.1
	Aspen (high priority)	0.00353	253	0.8
Watershed	Municipal watershed (DFC4)	0.00270	333	0.7
Diverse and resilient vegetation	Subalpine dry-mesic spruce-fir	0.00223	209	0.7
	Montane sagebrush steppe	0.00495	656	1.1
	Subalpine parkland	0.00131	171	0.6
	Subalpine wet-mesic spruce-fir	0.00285	266	0.8
	Aspen forest and woodland	0.00361	171	0.8
	Montane Douglas-fir	0.00343	266	0.8
Timber base	Desired Future Condition 1B	0.00264	245	0.8
	Desired Future Condition 10	0.00366	314	0.8

USDA Forest Service Gen. Tech. Rep. RMRS-GTR-315. 2013

63

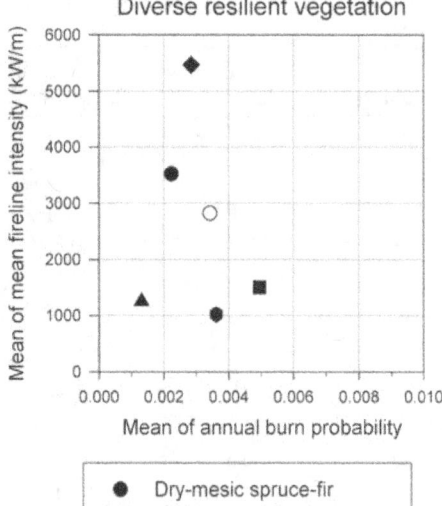

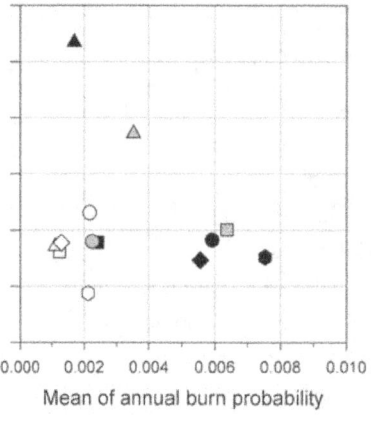

Figure 2☐—Exposure of the Diverse Resilient Vegetation, Wildlife Habitat and Priority Vegetation HVRAs to wildfire on the Bridger-Teton National Forest. Y-axis is the near-maximum fireline intensity (97th percentile condition).

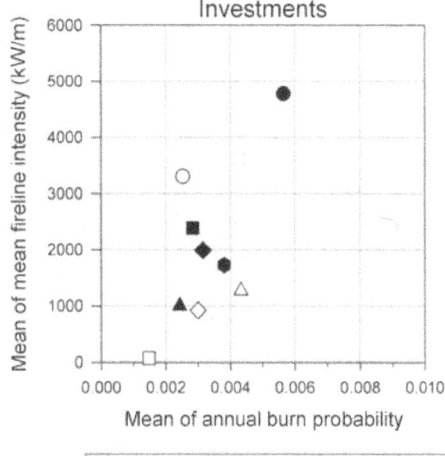

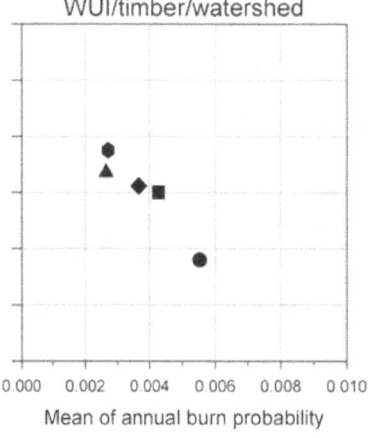

Figure 2☐—Exposure of the Investments, WUI, Timber and Watershed HVRAs to wildfire on the Bridger-Teton National Forest. Y-axis is the near-maximum fireline intensity (97th percentile condition).

64

USDA Forest Service Gen. Tech. Rep. RMRS-GTR-315. 2013

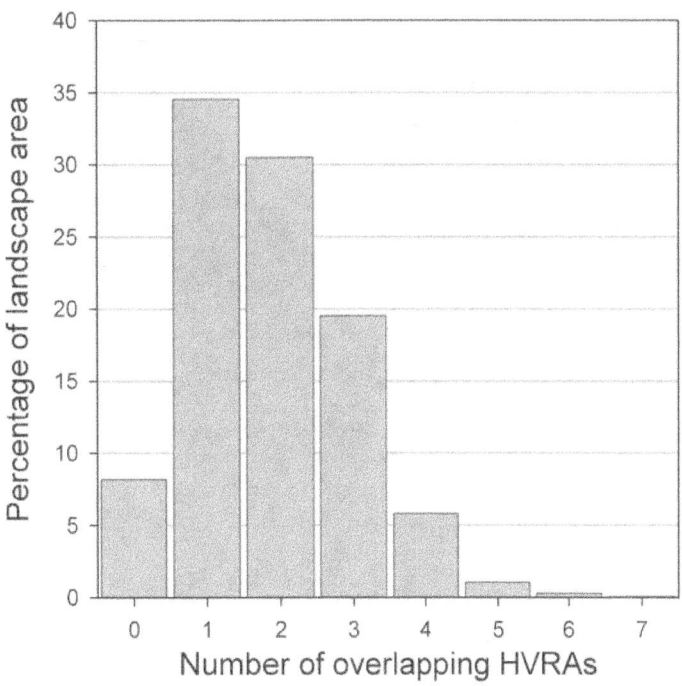

Figure ☐☐—Distribution of the number of overlapping HVRAs across the Bridger-Teton National Forest.

E(*wNVC*) was calculated using Equation 2 and summed across all HVRAs. The results are spatially displayed, with a logarithmic scale (log₁₀) used for the results (Figure 31). Each class of threat or benefit is an order of magnitude (10 times) greater than the previous. E(*wNVC*) combines information about wildfire hazard (burn probability by flame-length class) with information about the susceptibility, importance and extent of HVRAs. Positive values indicate that wildfire is expected to have a net positive effect; negative values indicate that wildfire is expected to have a net negative effect. The magnitude of the response values indicates the strength of the effect, whether positive or negative. These results show only the net effect; whether any offsetting effects are present are not indicated here.

The sum and mean E(*wNVC*) values—integrated wildfire risk—are shown for each HVRA in Table 22. The WUI defense zone has the greatest cumulative wildfire risk; the WUI protection zone accounts for just 7 percent as much risk. Sage grouse habitat represents the next-most threatened HVRAs, with core areas accounting for about half of the WUI defense zone risk and habitat near leks accounting for about 40 percent as much. All of the WUI and Investments HVRAs exhibit a net negative expected response to wildfire; none of these HVRAs had positive response function values for any FIL. In contrast, the expected wildfire "risk" to the diverse resilient vegetation HVRAs is uniformly positive, indicating a net benefit of wildfire on restoring or maintaining vegetation structure in all biophysical settings on the BTNF.

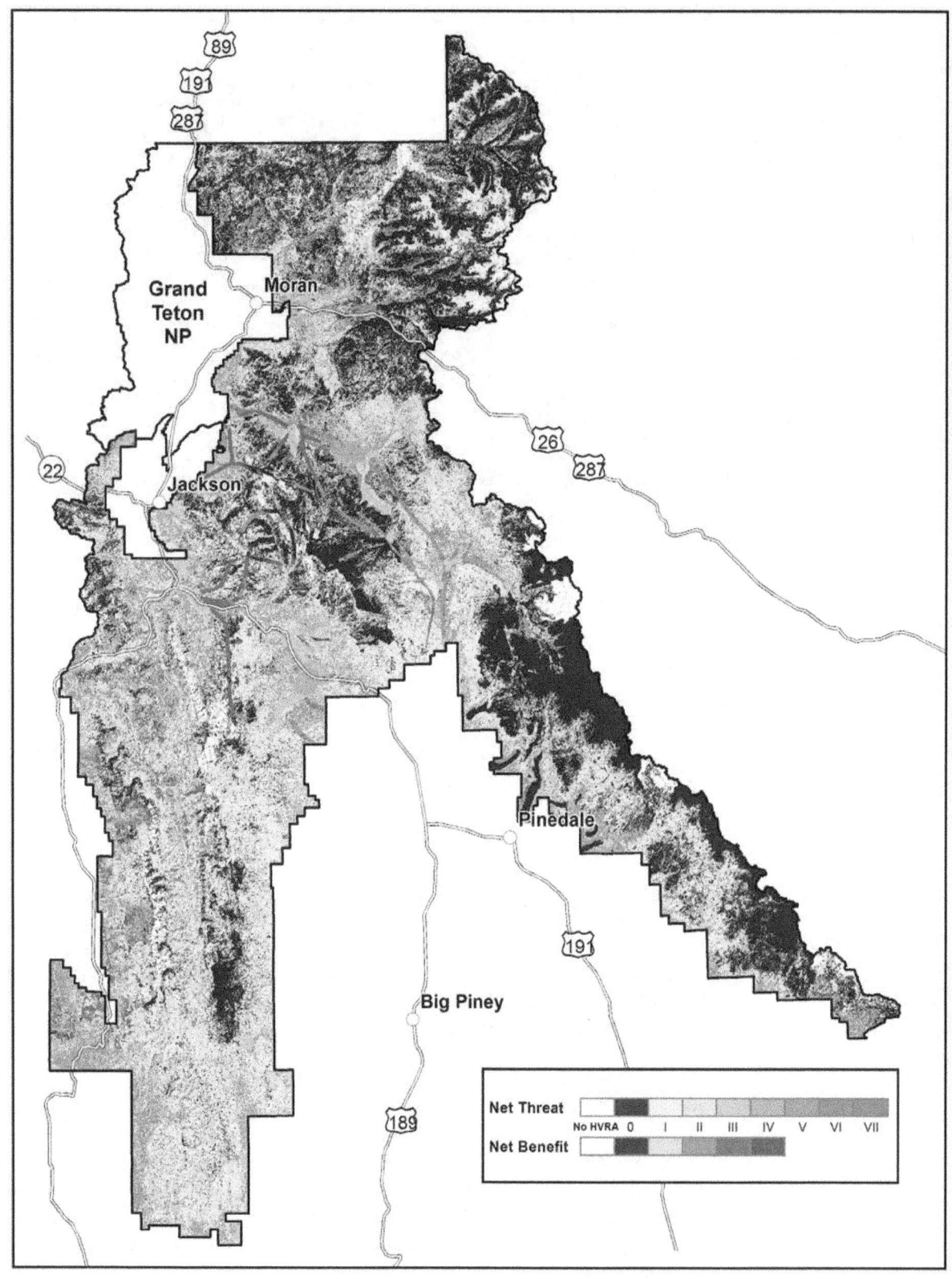

Figure □□—Weighted E(NVC) summed across all HVRAs on the BTNF. Values are displayed on a logarithmic scale (log10). Each category is an order of magnitude (10 times) greater than the previous.

Table 22—Weighted expected net value change [E(*wNVC*)] by HVRA on the Bridger–Teton National Forest. The sum of E(*wNVC*) is calculated by summing the E(*wNVC*) values for all grid cells of each sub–HVRA, and expressed as a percentage of the sub–HVRA with the greatest magnitude of *NVC* (whether positive or negative). For example, the WUI Protection FMU has 7.1 percent of the total risk of the WUI defense zone, which had the greatest magnitude of expected *NVC*. The mean E(*wNVC*) is the arithmetic mean of E(*wNVC*) values for all grid cells of a sub–HVRA, and is expressed on a logarithmic scale; a unit difference in values corresponds to a 10–fold difference in risk per unit area.

Primary	Sub–HVRA	Sum of E(*wNVC*)	Mean of E(*wNVC*)
		pct of max	log10
Investments	Feed grounds	−18.5	−6.9
	Special use permit areas	−13.2	−4.0
	Trailheads/boating sites	−1.6	−5.1
	Campgrounds/picnic areas	−2.4	−4.6
	Cabins/guard stations/lookouts	−18.3	−6.7
	Oil and gas development areas	−4.4	−3.3
	Communication sites	−0.8	−6.1
	Power lines	−9.9	−3.8
	White bark pine plus trees	−6.5	−6.6
WUI	WUI defense zone	−100.0	−3.7
	Protection FMU	−7.1	−2.4
Critical fish and wildlife habitat	Pronghorn migration routes	6.9	3.0
	Bighorn migration routes	15.0	3.2
	Moose thermal cover	3.1	2.7
	Sage grouse core areas	−55.0	−4.8
	Sage grouse near leks	−38.2	−4.1
	Trout and chub streams	2.6	1.2
Priority vegetation	Whitebark pine A	−4.7	−2.3
	Whitebark pine B	−0.8	−1.4
	Whitebark pine C	−3.9	−2.2
	Whitebark pine D	0.0	——
	Sensitive plants	−0.1	−0.2
	Feedground Aspen	−1.3	−3.0
	Aspen (high priority)	11.8	3.4
Watershed	Municipal watershed (DFC4)	−0.4	−1.7
Diverse and resilient vegetation	Subalpine dry–mesic spruce–fir	1.0	0.7
	Montane sagebrush steppe	1.3	2.3
	Subalpine parkland	1.3	1.3
	Subalpine wet–mesic spruce–fir	0.8	1.2
	Aspen forest and woodland	3.3	1.8
	Montane Douglas–fir	5.4	2.3
Timber base	Desired Future Condition 1B	−1.8	−1.8
	Desired Future Condition 10	3.2	1.4

USDA Forest Service Gen. Tech. Rep. RMRS-GTR-315. 2013

67

Dividing the cumulative risk to an HVRA by the land area it covers produces the mean risk per unit area. The resulting values vary over several orders of magnitude, so we present the results on a logarithmic scale (Table 22). Taken as a whole, the Investments HVRAs have the greatest risk per unit area, followed by the sage grouse HVRAs. The WUI defense zone, despite its status as the most-threatened HVRA, has less risk per unit area than the Investments, primarily because it covers so much more land area. The concentration of risk is an important factor when considering risk mitigation activities, such as fuel treatment. Where risk is concentrated, less land area may need to be treated in order to mitigate that risk. Where risk is distributed more thinly, such as in the municipal watershed HVRA, more treatment effort may be necessary to accomplish the same level of mitigation.

The cumulative risk results can also be summarized by any geographic unit, such as ranger districts, fire management unit, watersheds, etc. Wildfire hazard and response characteristics were summarized among ranger districts of the BTNF (Table 23). HVRA area is the land area covered by at least one HVRA; a pixel with overlapping HVRAs is counted only once. Expected annual area burned is the land area covered by at least one HVRA that is expected to burn annually; it is calculated as the product of HVRA area and mean BP. Mean BP is the arithmetic mean BP of the pixels covered by at least one HVRA. Finally, the last three columns in this table represent the cumulative weighted wildfire response results. The 'Benefit' column is the weighted positive value change among the ranger districts, without considering any offsetting negative effects. The 'threat' column is the weighted negative value change, without considering any offsetting positive effects. The values in these two columns are scaled such that the ranger district with the greatest positive or negative NVC is scaled to 100 or -100, respectively. The final column represents the sum of E($wNVC$) in each district.

These three basic measures—benefit, threat, and net response—can be summarized to illustrate how the overall response is distributed among HVRAs. The net response results for each HVRA (and sub-HVRA) are sorted by decreasing threat and displayed on a bar chart (Figure 32). Negative response is shown as a red bar; positive response is shown as a green bar. On the BTNF, the WUI defense zone is the HVRA with the greatest weighted net threat, so it is given a value of -100. The next most-threatened HVRAs are sage grouse core areas and sage grouse habitat near leks, which exhibit 55 percent and 38 percent of the threat represented by the WUI defense zone. As an example of the effect of offsetting threats and benefits, note that power lines and the WUI

Table 23—Wildfire hazard and cumulative weighted wildfire response across all HVRAs by BTNF ranger district.

BTNF Ranger District	HVRA area (ha)	Expected annual area burned (ha)	Mean burn prob. (fraction)	Benefit (+VC)	Threat (–VC)	Risk (NVC)
Big Piney RD	423,360	1,435	0.0034	9	–78	–69
Buffalo RD	334,786	643	0.0019	5	–12	–7
Greys River RD	329,569	1,042	0.0032	20	–21	–1
Jackson RD	422,881	1,414	0.0033	24	–100	–76
Kemmerer RD	317,642	1,238	0.0039	5	–12	–6
Pinedale RD	757,325	1,337	0.0018	8	–33	–26
non–Forest	4,227	15	0.0035	0	–11	–11

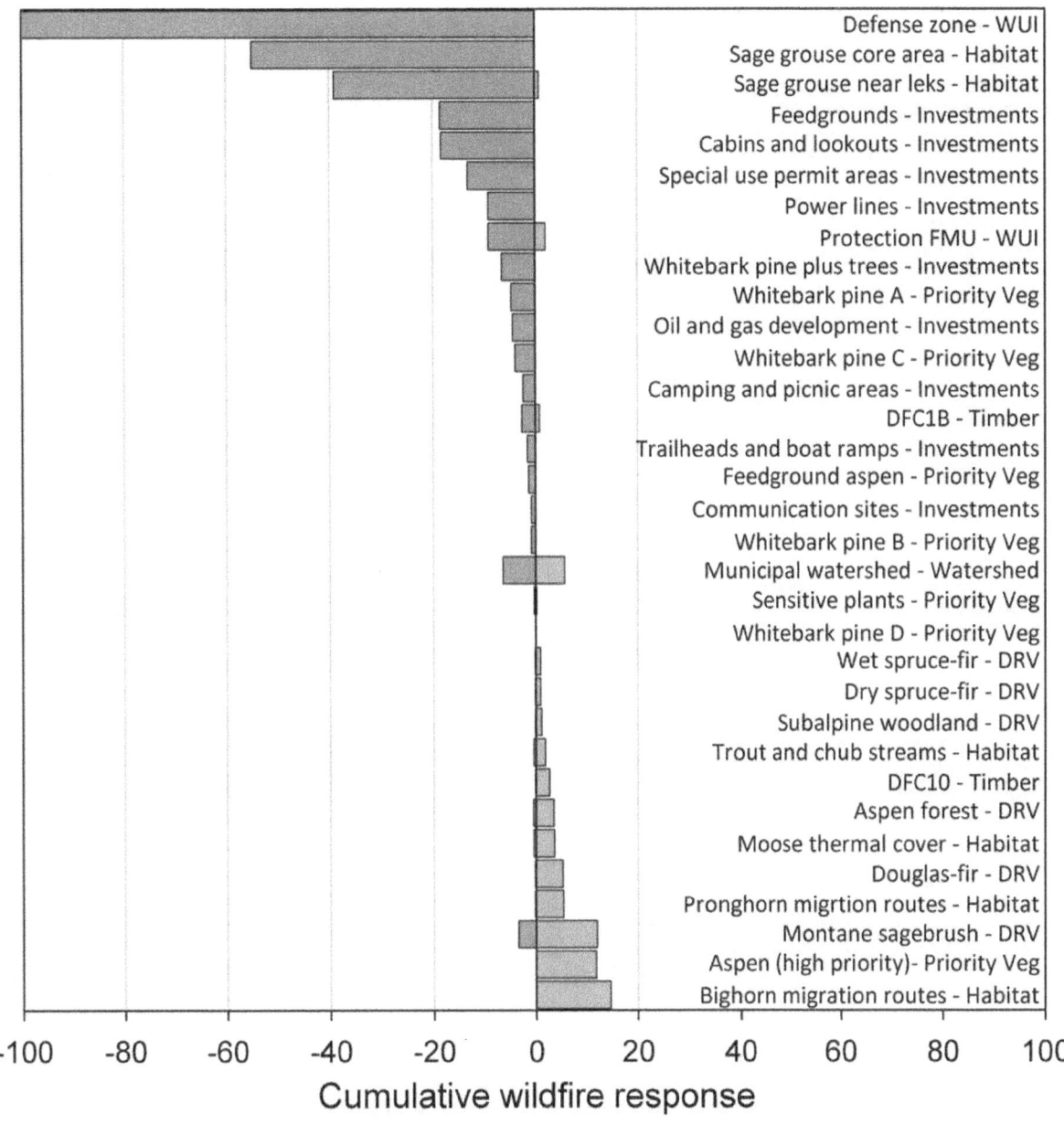

Figure 2—Weighted net response over all highly valued resources and assets (HVRAs) on the BTNF. HVRAs are listed in order from greatest expected negative net response at the top to greatest net benefit at the bottom.

protection zone have equal threat values (as represented on the x-axis), but the WUI protection zone has a different net response value (7 percent vs. 9 percent as represented in parentheses on the y-axis). This is because the response function for the protection zone indicates a small benefit of burning at low flame lengths, indicated by the small blue bar. The municipal watershed HVRA exhibits both positive and negative effects (at different flame lengths), but these effects are almost completely offsetting. Twelve of the 22 HVRAs exhibit a net positive response to wildfire, including all of the biophysical settings in the diverse and resilient vegetation HVRA. Note that the overall net positive effects are generally smaller in magnitude than the negative effects.

USDA Forest Service Gen. Tech. Rep. RMRS-GTR-315. 2013

69

8. Putting it All Together: Understanding and Managing Risk _____

At this point, the major components of a spatial wildfire risk assessment framework have been discussed. Wildfire risk assessment is premised on the analysis of exposure and effects, and on the estimation of wildfire likelihood, wildfire intensity, and HVRA response to wildfire. The assessment process we illustrated relies on burn probability modeling, the use of expert judgment to characterize HVRA-specific fire effects, and if necessary the articulation of relative importance weights across different HVRAs. These processes entail geospatial calculations that are performed on a pixel-by-pixel basis and summarized across the assessment landscape. Combining fire modeling outputs with HVRA-specific information (location, response, and relative importance) yields valuable information regarding expected net value change to individual HVRAs as well as integrated, weighted risk scores across all HVRAs of interest (Figure 33). Risk calculations can be displayed in graphical and tabular formats to help fire managers better understand how risks are distributed across the landscapes they manage.

The basic building block of the entire assessment process is burn probability modeling and the use of fire modeling outputs. Understanding the likely patterns of wildfire and its interactions with HVRAs (in other words, exposure analysis) is a critical first step to developing risk mitigation strategies. Integrating fire behavior models and geospatial analysis, therefore, can help directly inform risk mitigation and fuel management planning (Ager and others 2011). Further incorporating HVRA-specific response functions can capture differential responses to fire across HVRAs, both in terms of varying magnitudes of likely loss, as well as potential fire-related benefits for many ecological HVRAs. The additional integration of relative importance weights allows for comparison of landscape areas with a common measure, and can help inform prioritization of high risk areas.

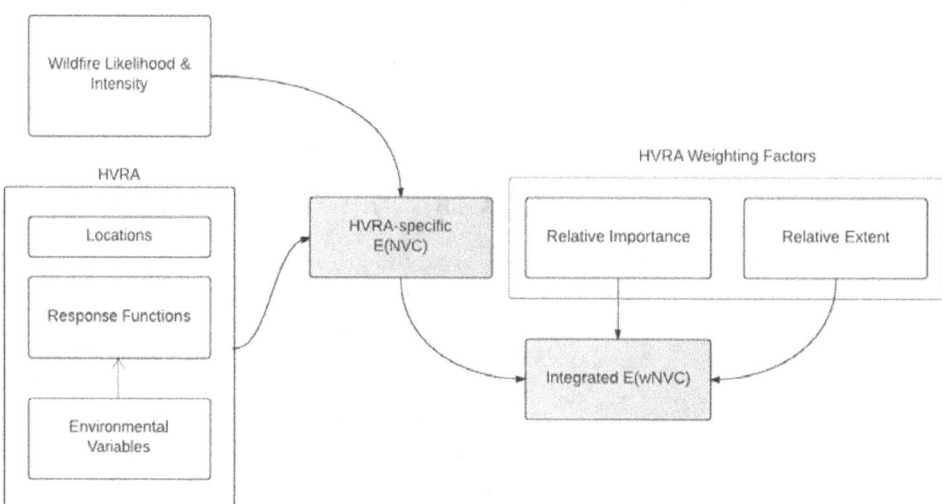

Figure ☐☐—Components of the risk assessment framework are combined to yield HVRA-specific risk scores as well as integrated, weighted risk scores across multiple HVRAs.

Figure 34 presents a conceptual model for analyzing interactions between wildfire management actions, wildfire likelihood and intensity, and the consequences of wildfire (including both benefits and losses). Use of this model can help explore how alternative land and fire management actions may reduce risks. These actions could include pre-fire investments in ignition prevention programs, response capacity, and hazardous fuels reduction, as well as changes in strategic incident response. Reducing HVRA exposure is also possible for a limited set of HVRAs such as human development or newly constructed infrastructure, and then only by not building the asset in a hazardous location in the first place. Controlling exposure is generally not possible for natural and cultural resources. This basic analytical framework can be brought to bear for strategic identification and comparison of wildfire risk mitigation options.

Further critical for examination and prioritization of risk mitigation strategies is the consideration of wildfire management objectives and management opportunities (Figure 35). The former will dictate the degree to which wildfire management emphasizes restoration or protection of HVRAs, and will likely exert significant influence on the design of both fuel treatment and suppression strategies. The latter relates to spatial and temporal constraints such as prescribed burning windows and land designations, operational constraints such as limitations for mechanical equipment, financial constraints relating to management costs, and could include broader sociopolitical concerns such as public support, all of which will vary with the nature and scope of the planning context.

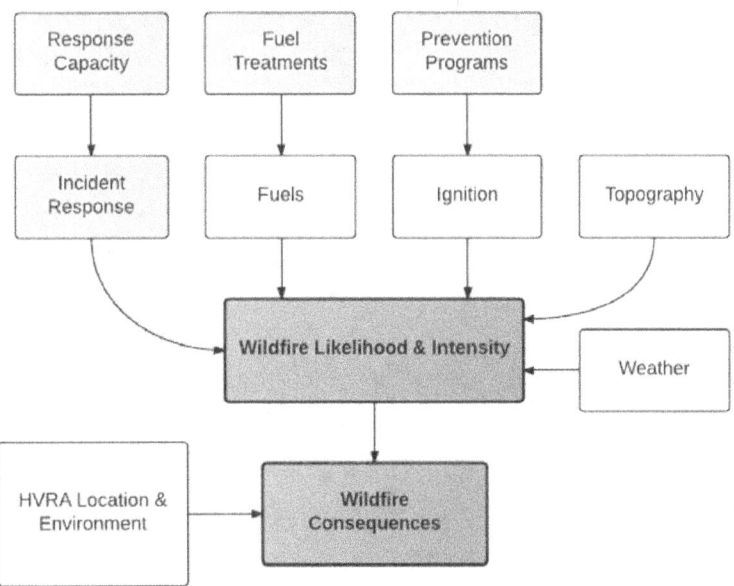

Figure □4—Conceptual model of wildfire management actions and their relation to primary factors driving wildfire risk. Boxes in light gray are management actions, and boxes in dark grey are assessment outputs. Figure modified from Calkin and others (2011a).

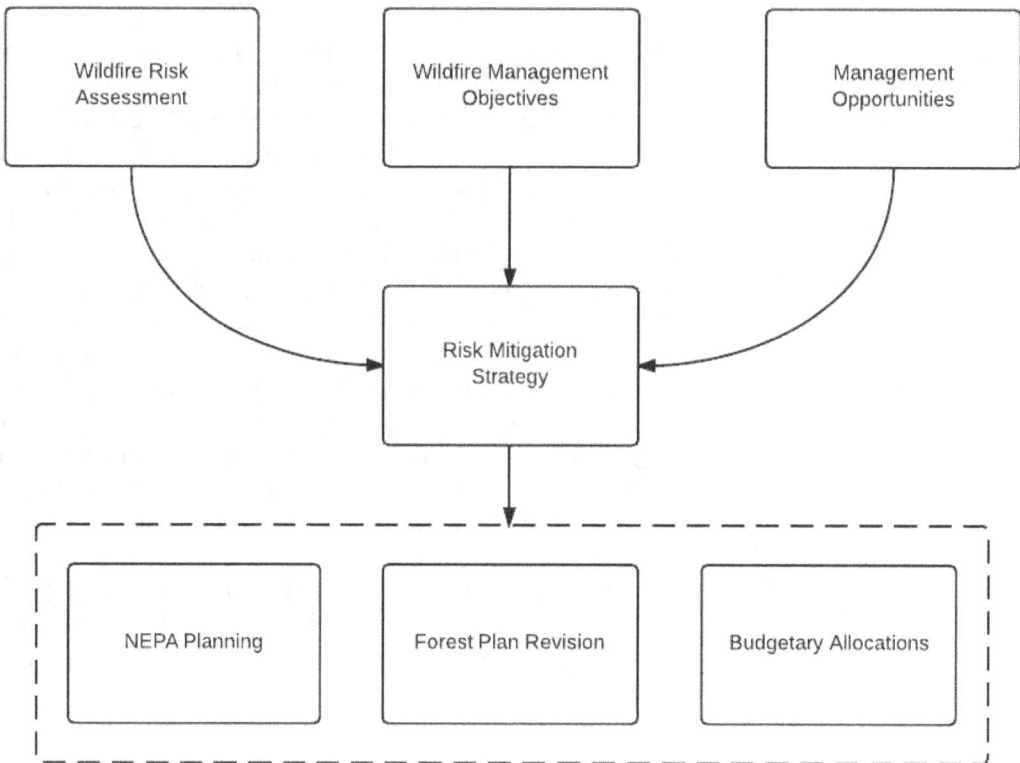

Figure ☐☐—Combining risk assessment, management objectives, and management opportunities can lead to development of risk mitigation strategies. Here three examples of different planning contexts are illustrated within the dashed-line box.

Principles of Wildfire Risk Assessment

- States scope of assessment and HVRAs

- Incorporates spatial information on wildfire likelihood, intensity, and effects

- Discloses data sources, methods, logic, and rationale

- Articulates major assumptions and uncertainties

- Separates science-based from value-based and policy-based judgments

- Expresses results clearly and concisely

9. Discussion and Conclusions

Assessing wildfire risk is a crucial component of wildfire management and risk mitigation planning. A spatial, quantitative characterization of wildfire risk allows for identification of areas on the landscape where aggressive treatment might be cost-effective, or alternatively where fire may play a benign or even beneficial role and could be encouraged rather than suppressed. This information could prove useful for the preparation of fire management plans, the delineation of FMUs, and development of corresponding fire response objectives. The definition of HVRA response as a function of fire behavior facilitates the design of fuel treatments to ameliorate undesirable or encourage desirable fire intensities. Including landscape variables into the response functions (in addition to the baseline fire intensity) can improve response function definitions.

Wildfire risk assessment results provide a snapshot of current landscape conditions and associated risks. Periodic assessment over time can provide critical information for monitoring trends in risk and evaluating the performance of previous risk mitigation investments. It is also possible to modify assessment inputs (for example, fuel conditions) to reassess risks in a comparative risk assessment framework to evaluate the likely cost-effectiveness of future mitigation investments.

Two great strengths of the risk assessment framework described herein are its flexibility and its scalability. The framework is quite flexible in the sense that the set of HVRAs to be included, the response function definitions, and additional environmental variables influencing HVRA response can vary widely from analysis to analysis. Further, although we illustrated a specific assessment process here, the general framework incorporating fire likelihood, intensity, and effects can be implemented in a variety of ways. The framework is scalable in the sense that the basic framework can be applied at project level all the way to national scale planning.

Key factors influencing the success of risk assessment efforts are the level of resources committed and the sufficiency and availability of scale-appropriate geospatial data. A fundamental component of the assessment framework is geospatial analysis and, in our experience, a necessary first step is to establish clear and consistent definitions of geospatial data (fire and fuels data in addition to HVRA data). Only then can the assessment proceed to wildfire modeling, HVRA fire effects analysis, and HVRA relative importance articulation. It can be helpful to devote time for pre-workshop training to familiarize participants with the processes of defining response functions and relative importance weights.

It is important to explicitly recognize key sources of uncertainty and to clearly document assessment data and processes. The predominant role of fire modeling in the assessment process points to a need for careful calibration and critique of fire modeling inputs (for example, fire behavior fuel models and canopy characteristics) and outputs (for example, burn probabilities). The proposed reliance on formality and documentation in the elicitation of expert input for both response functions and relative importance weights enables transparency and future external review of risk assessment results. Further, the explicit separation of fire effects from management priorities avoids potential pitfalls of conflating science-based and values-based information, or from "gaming" the assessment to achieve desired results.

In summary, the risk assessment framework and toolkit presented in this report provides for a systematic, transparent, and understandable approach to evaluating and mitigating the likely consequences of wildfire. The framework has already been applied in a variety of locations, at a variety of scales, and in a variety of planning contexts. We anticipate further adoption of the framework as fire managers become comfortable with risk management and as modelers and analysts become comfortable with burn probability modeling techniques. Research and development will continue to refine our abilities to understand and quantify wildfire risk. Implementing this risk assessment framework in the meantime is another step in the direction of risk-informed fire management to best achieve land and resource objectives.

Acknowledgments

Funding for the production of this report was provided by the National Fire Decision Support Center; initial funding for development of some risk assessment concepts presented here was provided by the Western Wildland Environmental Threat Assessment Center. Alan Ager and Mark Finney were both integrally involved in the development and advancement of wildfire exposure and risk concepts, without which this report would not be possible. We thank Julie Gilbertson-Day (Rocky Mountain Research Station), Don Helmbrecht (TEAMS Enterprise Unit), Eva Karau (Fire Modeling Institute) and Rick Stratton (Pacific Northwest Region) for their helpful review comments. We thank Martha Williamson (Bridger-Teton National Forest) for her assistance in implementing the example risk assessment used in this report.

References

Ager, A.A.; Finney, M. A.; Kerns, B. K.; Maffei, H. 2007. Modeling wildfire risk to northern spotted owl (*Strix occidentalis caurina*) habitat in Central Oregon, USA. Forest Ecology and Management. 246(1): 45-56.

Ager, A.A.; Vaillant, N. M.; Finney, M. A. 2010. A comparison of landscape fuel treatment strategies to mitigate wildland fire risk in the urban interface and preserve old forest structure. Forest Ecology and Management. 259(8): 1556-1570.

Ager, A.A.; Vaillant, N.M.; Finney, M.A. 2011. Integrating fire behavior models and geospatial analysis for wildland fire risk assessment and fuel management planning. Journal of Combustion. Article ID 572452: doi: 1155/2011/572452.

Ager, A. A.; Vaillant, N. M.; Finney, M. A.; Preisler, H. K. 2012. Analyzing wildfire exposure and source-sink relationships on a fire prone forest landscape. Forest Ecology and Management. 267: 271-283.

Albini, F. A. 1976. Estimating wildfire behavior and effects. Gen. Tech. Rep. INT-30. Ogden, UT: U.S. Department of Agriculture, Forest Service, Intermountain Forest and Range Experiment Station. 92 p.

Ananda, J.; Herath, G. 2009. A critical review of multi-criteria decision making methods with special reference to forest management and planning. Ecological Economics. 68: 2535-2548.

Andrews, P. L.; Loftsgaarden, D. O.; Bradshaw, L. S. 2003. Evaluation of fire danger rating indexes using logistic regression and percentile analysis. International Journal of Wildland Fire. 12(2): 213-226.

Ascough, J. C., II; Maier, H. R.; Ravalico, J. K.; Strudley, M. W. 2008. Future research challenges for incorporation of uncertainty in environmental and ecological decision-making. Ecological Modelling. 219(3): 383-399.

Bar Massada, A.; Radeloff, V. C.; Stewart, S. I.; Hawbaker, T. J. 2009. Wildfire risk in the wildland-urban interface: a simulation study in northwestern Wisconsin. Forest Ecology and Management. 258(9): 1990-1999.

Byram, G. M. 1959. Combustion of forest fuels. In: Forest fire: control and use, 2nd edition. New York: McGraw-Hill: 61–89.

Calkin, D. E.; Ager, A. A.; Thompson, M. P. 2011a. A comparative risk assessment framework for wildland fire management: the 2010 cohesive strategy science report. Gen. Tech. Rep. RMRS-GTR-262. Fort Collins, CO: U.S. Department of Agriculture, Forest Service, Rocky Mountain Research Station. 63 p.

Calkin, D. E.; Thompson, M. P.; Finney, M. A.; Hyde, K. D. 2011b. A real-time risk-assessment tool supporting wildland fire decision-making. Journal of Forestry. 109(5): 274-280.

Campbell, R. B.; Bartos, D. L. 2001. Aspen ecosystems: objectives for sustaining biodiversity. In: Shepperd, W. D., Binkley, D., Bartos, D.L., Stohlgren, T.J., Eskew, L.G. (Eds.), Sustaining aspen in western landscapes: Symposium proceedings. Proc. RMRS-P-18. Fort Collins, CO: U.S. Department of Agriculture, Forest Service, Rocky Mountain Research Station: 299–307.

Cannon, S. H.; Gartner, J. E.; Rupert, M. G.; Michael, J. A.; Rea, A. H.; Parrett, C. 2010. Predicting the probability and volume of postwildfire debris flows in the intermountain western United States. Geological Society of America Bulletin. 122(1-2): 127-144.

Catchpole, E. A.; De Mestre, N. J.; Gill, A. M. 1982. Intensity of fire at its perimeter. Australian Forest Research. 12: 47-54.

Crosby, J. S.; Chandler, C. C. 1966. Get the most from your windspeed observation. Fire Control Notes. 27(4): 12-13.

Cruz, M. G.; Alexander, M. E.; Wakimoto, R. H. 2005. Development and testing of models for predicting crown fire rate of spread in conifer forest stands. Canadian Journal of Forest Research. 35(7): 1626-1639.

Fairbrother, A.; Turnley, J. G. 2005. Predicting risks of uncharacteristic wildfires: application of the risk assessment process. Forest Ecology and Management. 211(1): 28-35.

Finney, M. A. 1998. FARSITE: Fire Area Simulator—model development and evaluation. Res. Pap. RMRS-RP-4. Fort Collins, CO: U.S. Department of Agriculture, Forest Service, Rocky Mountain Research Station. 47 p.

Finney, M. A. 2005. The challenge of quantitative risk analysis for wildland fire. Forest Ecology and Management. 211(1): 97-108.

Finney, M. A. 2006. An overview of FlamMap fire modeling capabilities. In: Andrews, P.L., Butler, B.W. (Comps). Fuels management-how to measure success: conference proceedings; March 28–30; Portland, OR. Proc. RMRS-P-41. Fort Collins, CO: U.S. Department of Agriculture, Forest Service, Rocky Mountain Research Station: 213–220.

Finney, M. A.; Grenfell, I. C.; McHugh, C. W.; Seli, R. C.; Tretheway, D.; Stratton, R. D.; Britton, S. 2011a. A method for ensemble wildland fire simulation. Environmental Modeling and Assessment. 16: 153-167.

Finney, M. A.; McHugh, C. W.; Grenfell, I. C.; Riley, K. L.; Short, K. C. 2011b. A simulation of probabilistic wildfire risk components for the continental United States. Stochastic Environmental Research and Risk Assessment. 25(7): 973-1000.

Gregory, R.; Long, G. 2009. Using structured decision making to help implement a precautionary approach to endangered species management. Risk Analysis. 29(4): 518-532.

Haas, J. R.; Calkin, D. E.; Thompson, M. P. 2013. A national approach for integrating wildfire simulation modeling into Wildland Urban Interface risk assessments within the United States. Landscape and Urban Planning. 119: 44-53.

Helmbrecht, D.; Scott, J. H.; Keefe, D. 2012. Little Belts landscape assessment: vegetation departure and wildfire threat report. Unpublished report on file at: . U.S. Department of Agriculture, Forest Service, Lewis and Clark National Forest Supervisor's Office, Great Falls, MT.

Helmbrecht, D.; Williamson, M.; Abendroth, D. 2013. Bridger-Teton National Forest vegetation condition assessment. Unpublished report on file at: U.S. Department of Agriculture, Forest Service, Bridger-Teton National Forest Supervisor's Office, Jackson, WY.

Hyde, K.; Dickinson, M. B.; Bohrer, G.; Calkin, D.; Evers, L.; Gilbertson-Day, J.; Nicolet, T.; Ryan, K.; Tague, C. 2013. Research and development supporting risk-based wildfire effects prediction for fuels and fire management: status and needs. International Journal of Wildland Fire. 22: 37-50.

Kiker, G. A.; Bridges, T. S.; Varghese, A.; Seager, T. P.; Linkov, I. 2005. Application of multicriteria decision analysis in environmental decision making. Integrated Environmental Assessment and Management. 1(2): 95-108.

Knol, A. B.; Slottje, P.; van der Sluijs, J. P.; Lebret, E. 2010. The use of expert elicitation in environmental health impact assessment: a seven step procedure. Environmental Health. 9(1): 19.

Kuhnert, P. M.; Martin, T. G.; Griffiths, S. P. 2010. A guide to eliciting and using expert knowledge in Bayesian ecological models. Ecology Letters. 13(7): 900-914.

Loosen, A. S.; Kilpatrick, S.; Graham, M.; Younkin, B. 2009. Aspen assessment and inventory in the Greys River Ranger District final report. Jackson, WY: Conservation Research Center of Teton Science Schools.

MacMillan, D.C.; Marshall, K. 2006. The Delphi process – an expert-based approach to ecological modelling and data-poor environments. Animal Conservation. 9(1): 11-19.

Marcot, B. G.; Thompson, M. P.; Runge, M. C.; Thompson, F. R.; McNulty, S.; Cleaves, D.; Tomosy, M.; Fisher, L. A.; Bliss, A. 2012. Recent advances in applying decision science to managing national forests. Forest Ecology and Management. 285(1): 123-132.

Miller, C.; Ager, A. A. 2012. A review of recent advances in risk analysis for wildfire management. International Journal of Wildland Fire. 22: 1-14.

Morgan, M. G.; Henrion, M. 1990. Uncertainty: a guide to dealing with uncertainty in quantitative risk and policy analysis. New York: Cambridge University Press.

Noonan-Wright, E.; Opperman, T. S.; Finney, M. A.; Zimmerman, T. G.; Seli, R. C.; Elenz, L. M; Calkin, D. E.; Fiedler, J. R. 2011. Developing the U.S. Wildland Fire Decision Support System (WFDSS). Journal of Combustion. 2011: Article ID 168473: doi: 10.1155/2011/168473. 14 p.

Peterson, D. L.; Evers, L.; Gravenmier, R. A.; Eberhardt, E. 2007. A consumer guide: tools to manage vegetation and fuels. Gen. Tech. Rep. PNW-GTR-690. Portland, OR: U.S. Department of Agriculture, Forest Service, Pacific Northwest Research Station. 151 p.

Radeloff, V. C.; Hammer, R. B.; Stewart, S. I.; Fried, J. S.; Holcomb. S. S.; McKeefry, J. F. 2005. The Wildland Urban Interface in the United States. Ecological Applications. 15: 799-805.

Reinhardt, E. D.; Dickinson, M. B. 2010. First-order fire effects models for land management: overview and issues. Fire Ecology. 6(1): 131-142.

Roose, H.; Ballard, L.; Manley, J.; Saleen, N.; Harbert, S. 2008. Fire Program Analysis System—Preparedness Module. In: González-Cabán, A., (Tech. Ed.) Proceedings of the second international symposium on fire economics, planning, and policy: a global view. Gen. Tech. Rep. PSW-GTR-208 (English). Albany, CA: U.S. Department of Agriculture, Forest Service, Pacific Southwest Research Station: 377-384.

Rothermel, R. C. 1972. A mathematical model for predicting fire spread in wildland fuels. Res. Pap. INT-115. Ogden, UT: U.S. Department of Agriculture, Forest Service, Intermountain Forest and Range Experiment Station. 40 p.

Rothermel, R. C. 1991. Predicting behavior and size of crown fires in the Northern Rocky Mountains. Res. Pap. INT-438. Ogden, UT: U.S. Department of Agriculture, Forest Service, Intermountain Forest and Range Experiment Station. 46 p.

Scott, J. H. 2006. An analytical framework for quantifying wildland fire risk and fuel treatment benefit. In: Andrews, P.L., Butler, B.W. (Comps.), Fuels management—how to measure success: conference proceedings; March 28–30; Portland, OR. Proc. RMRS-P-41. Fort Collins, CO: U.S. Department of Agriculture, Forest Service, Rocky Mountain Research Station: 169–184.

Scott J. H. 2007. Hazard. In: FireWords: Fire Science Glossary [electronic]. U. S. Department of Agriculture, Forest Service, Rocky Mountain Research Station, Fire Sciences Laboratory (Producer). Available: www.firewords.net.

Scott, J. H.; Burgan, R. E. 2005. Standard fire behavior fuel models: a comprehensive set for use with Rothermel's surface fire spread model. Gen. Tech. Rep. RMRS-GTR-153. Fort. Collins, CO: U.S. Department of Agriculture, Forest Service, Rocky Mountain Research Station. 72 p.

Scott, J. H.; Helmbrecht, D. 2010. Wildfire threat to key resources on the Beaverhead-Deerlodge National Forest. Unpublished report on file at: U.S. Department of Agriculture, Forest Service, Beaverhead-Deerlodge National Forest Supervisor's Office, Butte, MT. 44 p.

Scott, J. H.; Helmbrecht, D. J.; Parks, S. A.; Miller, C. 2012a. Quantifying the threat of unsuppressed wildfires reaching adjacent wildland-urban interface on the Bridger-Teton National Forest, Wyoming, USA. Fire Ecology. 8(2): 125-142.

Scott, J. H.; Helmbrecht, D. J.; Thompson, M. P.; Calkin, D. E.; Marcille, K. 2012b. Probabilistic assessment of wildfire hazard and municipal watershed exposure. Natural Hazards. 64(1): 707-728.

Scott, J. H.; Helmbrecht D.; Williamson, M. 2013. Response of highly valued resources and assets to wildfire within Grand Teton National Park and the Bridger-Teton National Forest. Unpublished report on file at: U.S. Department of Agriculture, Forest Service, Bridger-Teton National Forest Supervisor's Office, Jackson, WY.

Scott, J. H.; Reinhardt, E. D. 2001. Assessing crown fire potential by linking models of surface and crown fire behavior. Res. Pap. RMRS-RP-29. Fort Collins, CO: U.S. Department of Agriculture, Forest Service, Rocky Mountain Research Station. 59 p.

Short, K. C. 2013. A spatial database of wildfires in the United States, 1992-2011. Earth System Science Data Discussion. 6: 297-366. doi:10.5194/essdd-6-297-2013.

Stratton, R. D. 2006. Guidance on spatial wildland fire analysis: models, tools, and techniques. Gen. Tech. Rep. RMRS-GTR-183. Fort Collins, CO: U.S. Department of Agriculture, Forest Service, Rocky Mountain Research Station. 15 p.

Stratton, R. D. 2009. Guidebook on LANDFIRE fuels data acquisition, critique, modification, maintenance, and model calibration. Gen. Tech. Rep. RMRS-GTR-220. Fort Collins, CO: U.S. Department of Agriculture, Forest Service, Rocky Mountain Research Station. 54 p.

Strauss, D.; Bednar, L.; Mees, R. 1989. Do one percent of the forest fires cause ninety-nine percent of the damage? Forest Science. 35(2): 319-328.

Thomas, P. H. 1963. The size of flames from natural fires. In: Proceedings of the ninth symposium on combustion; 1962. New York: Academic Press: 844–859.

Thompson, M. P.; Calkin, D. E. 2011. Uncertainty and risk in wildland fire management: a review. Journal of Environmental Management. 92(8): 1895-1909.

Thompson, M. P.; Calkin, D. E.; Finney, M. A.; Ager, A. A.; Gilbertson-Day, J. W. 2011. Integrated national-scale assessment of wildfire risk to human and ecological values. Stochastic Environmental Research and Risk Assessment. 25(6): 761-780.

Thompson, M. P.; Scott, J. H.; Helmbrecht, D.; Calkin, D. E. 2013a. Integrated wildfire risk assessment: framework development and application on the Lewis and Clark National Forest in Montana, USA. Integrated Environmental Assessment and Management. 9(2): 329-342.

Thompson, M. P.; Scott, J. H.; Langowski, P. G.; Gilbertson-Day, J. W.; Haas, J. R.; Bowne, E. M. 2013b. Assessing watershed-wildfire risks on National Forest System lands in the Rocky Mountain Region of the United States. Water. 5(3): 945-971.

USDA Forest Service. 1990. Bridger-Teton National Forest Land and resource management plan. Jackson, WY: U.S. Department of Agriculture, Forest Service, Region 4, Bridger-Teton National Forest.

USDA Forest Service. 2007. Existing vegetation mapping summary: Bridger-Teton National Forest. Tech. Rep. RSAC-0091-TECH1. Remote Sensing Applications Center. 128 pp.

USDA Forest Service. 2012. Bridger-Teton National Forest Fire Management Plan. Jackson, WY: U.S. Department of Agriculture, Region 4, Bridger-Teton National Forest.

Vaillant, N.M.; Ager, A.A.; Anderson. J. 2013. ArcFuels10 system overview. Gen. Tech. Rep. PNW-GTR-875. Portland, OR: U.S. Department of Agriculture, Forest Service, Pacific Northwest Research Station. 65p.

Van Wagner, C. E. 1977. Conditions for the start and spread of crown fire. Canadian Journal of Forest Research. 7(1): 23-34.

Venn, T. J.; Calkin, D. E. 2011. Accommodating non-market values in evaluation of wildfire management in the United States: challenges and opportunities. International Journal of Wildland Fire. 20(3): 327-339.

Appendix A—Acronyms and Variables

Acronyms

BTNF—Bridger-Teton National Forest
DFC—desired future condition
DRV—Diverse, resilient vegetation
ERC—Energy Release Component of the NFDRS
FIL—fire intensity level
FMP—Fire Management Plan
FMU—Fire Management Unit
FPA—Fire Program Analysis
GIS—geographic information system
GYCC—Greater Yellowstone Coordinating Committee
HUC—hydrologic unit code
HVRA—highly valued resource or asset
LCP—fire modeling landscape file
LRMP—Land and Resource Management Plan (Forest plan)
NEPA—National Environmental Policy Act
NFDRS—National Fire Danger Rating System
NFMA—National Forest Management Act
NAD—North American Datum
RAWS—Remote Automated Weather Station
RAVAR—Rapid Assessment of Values at Risk
RDPA—Residentially Developed Populated Areas
TIARA—Tetons Interagency Risk Assessment
WFDSS—Wildland Fire Decision Support System
WUI—wildland urban interface

Variables

BP—burn probability
CFL—conditional flame length
$E(NVC)$—expected value of NVC
$E(wNVC)$—expected value of weighted NVC
ERC—Energy Release Component of the NFDRS
ERC-G—ERC calculated using fuel model 'G'
FL—flame length
FLI—fireline intensity
FLP—flame-length probability
H—fuel particle low heat of combustion
MC—moisture content
MFI—mean fireline intensity
NVC—net value change
P_{LFD}—probability of a large-fire day
R—rate of spread
RE—relative extent
RI—relative importance
W_f—load of fuel consumed in the flaming fire front

USDA Forest Service Gen. Tech. Rep. RMRS-GTR-315. 2013

77

Appendix B—Glossary

It will be helpful to establish a common set of definitions and a common understanding of the various components of wildfire risk.

Asset

An asset is a man-made thing—a building, communication tower, road, etc.—of use or value to its owner. By contrast, resources are naturally occurring—wildlife habitat, forage, timber, etc. Assets and resources can be damaged by wildfire, resulting in reduction in value, or loss. Some resources increase in value after fire (a benefit of fire), but assets generally do not.

Benefit

An increase in the value of a resource or asset (although assets generally do not benefit from fire). The benefit to a resource may partially or wholly offset loss due to resource damage. The net effect of benefit and loss is called net value change (NVC), but has also been called net loss or net benefit.

Burn probability (*BP*)

The probability that a wildfire will burn a given point or area during a specified period of time. Burn probability for wildfire management planning applications is often reported on an annual basis—the probability of burning at any time during a single calendar year. Some planning applications report the conditional burn probability given that a fire occurs during a specified "problem fire" weather scenario. Wildfire incident management applications express burn probability for a much shorter time frame, typically one to four weeks. For practical purposes, wildfire simulation systems treat the burning of each pixel, the smallest landscape unit, as a point.

Conditional wildfire intensity

The typical wildfire intensity produced by the fire environment at a point, incorporating non-heading spread directions and the full range of weather scenarios. Two measures of wildfire intensity are in common use—flame length and fireline intensity. Flame length is commonly used in contemporary wildfire hazard and threat assessments. When using a Monte Carlo wildfire simulation system, conditional flame length (CFL) is the mean flame length of the iterations that burned a particular landscape pixel. The FSIM wildfire simulation system also produces an output raster for mean fireline intensity—the mean fireline intensity of the iterations that burned each landscape pixel. Conditional wildfire intensity refers to the contemporary, not historical, typical wildfire intensity. *See also:* conditional flame length *(CFL),* mean fireline intensity *(MFI).*

Conditional flame length (*CFL*)

The mean flame length at a point, quantified as the mean flame length simulated with a Monte Carlo fire occurrence simulator. Conditional flame length is one of two common measures of conditional wildfire intensity (the other is mean fireline intensity).

Conditional burn probability

Burn probability given a specific set of defining criteria. The specific criteria can be a weather scenario and a fixed, usually short period of active fire spread. Conditional burn probability is calculated for use in hazard and threat assessments that use Flam-Map5 rather than FSIM or FSPro. The flame length probabilities reported by FSim and FlamMap5 are conditional.

Damage

An adverse physical change of an asset or resource. Damage is physical change, not the effect of that change on value (that is *loss*). The consumption of a building, death of desirable trees in a forest stand, and degradation of air quality are example of damage a wildfire can cause. Damage can be direct or induced. Examples of direct wildfire damage include tree mortality and consumption of buildings. Examples of induced wildfire damages include reduction of forest productivity due to soil erosion and sedimentation of a reservoir.

Effects

The anticipated benefits and losses to HVRAs, typically quantified as a function of fire intensity.

Effects analysis

The analysis of likely HVRA response to wildfire (benefits and losses), typically quantified as a function of fire intensity. This analysis can incorporate preexisting HVRA-specific models, or, as implemented here, can rely on expert-based response functions. *See also: effects.*

Expected loss

See expected net value change.

Expected net value change

Expected net value change, or E(NVC), is calculated as the sum-product of burn probability and value change (to one or more resources or assets) over a range of wildfire intensity classes (usually flame length). Expected net value change is a risk-neutral measure of the wildfire risk to resources and assets, and forms the basis for the quantitative wildfire risk assessment process described in this report. If no beneficial effects are under consideration, expected net value change can simply be called expected loss. The terms value change, response and net response are functional synonyms for net value change; all refer to the net effects of positive and negative changes on the value of a resource or asset.

Expected value

Expected value is the probability-weighted average outcome, a good measure of the central tendency of outcomes. For example, if a system or simulation has a 90 percent probability of producing an outcome of 0, a 9 percent chance of an outcome of 10, and a one percent chance of an outcome of 1000, then the expected value is 10.9, as shown in the table below. Notice that 10.9 is not among the possible outcomes.

probability	outcome	Expected value
0.90	0	0
0.09	10	0.9
0.01	1000	10
1.00		10.9

USDA Forest Service Gen. Tech. Rep. RMRS-GTR-315. 2013

7

Exposure

The spatial coincidence of wildfire likelihood and intensity with the location of an HVRA. For example, a building (asset) in a flammable forest (hazard) is exposed to wildfire. Exposure can be intentional or incidental. A valuable but flammable forest is incidentally exposed to damage from wildfire, because the forest cannot be physically separated from the hazard. The construction of a residential building in the same flammable forest is intentional exposure to the same hazard.

Exposure analysis

An assessment of wildfire hazard—likelihood and intensity—where resources and assets are located.

Fire modeling landscape

A raster-format geospatial characterization of fuel (fire behavior fuel model, canopy base height, and canopy bulk density), vegetation (canopy cover and stand height) and topography (slope, aspect and elevation) needed to simulate potential fire behavior and fire growth across a landscape. For use in FlamMap5 and FSim, the fire modeling landscape must be in the form of an LCP file (Finney 1998).

Fire occurrence

An instance of a wildfire event; a wildfire incident. Fire occurrence is defined by the characteristics of historical wildfires occurring in a specified area during a specified period of time: frequency, density, start location, start date, fuel type, final size, management objective, and so on.

Fireline intensity (*FLI*)

The rate of heat release per unit length of flaming fire front, calculated as the product of heat content, fuel consumption during flaming front passage, and rate of spread.

Frequency

The number of occurrences per unit time.

Fuelscape

A raster-format geospatial characterization of ground, surface and canopy fuel across a landscape, typically consisting of one or more fuel characteristics data layers. For fire behavior modeling, a fuelscape consists of geospatial data layers representing surface fuel model, canopy base height and canopy bulk density. Other geospatial data layers required for geospatial fire modeling include topography characteristics (slope, aspect, elevation) and vegetation characteristics (forest canopy cover and height).

Grid cell

A grid cell—also called a pixel—is the smallest addressable unit in a raster dataset.

Harm

Injury to a person. Harm is analogous to *damage.* Damage occurs to anthropogenic or natural objects—assets or resources—whereas harm occurs to persons.

Hazard

A physical situation with potential for harm to persons or damage to resources and assets. Wildfire hazard can be described qualitatively as a fire environment—fuel, weather, topography, and ignitions—with potential for causing harm or damage, or quantitatively by two characteristics: (1) the probability of a fire occurring at a specific point during a specified time period, and (2) the expected distribution of intensity given that the event does occur. Wildfire hazard at a given location on the landscape is quantified as: (1) burn probability and (2) conditional wildfire intensity given that a fire does occur. Those two characteristics can be combined into a single spatially resolved measure of wildfire hazard: integrated wildfire hazard. It is important to note that since the definition of risk in the wildfire context is expanded to include beneficial as well as negative effects, the consideration of wildfire likelihood and intensity (in other words, hazard) should be expanded as well.

HVRA

Highly Valued Resource or Asset. Some resources have only modest value and may not be analyzed in an assessment of risk to HVRAs. Likewise, low-value assets like outbuildings are often left un-analyzed so that efforts can be focused on the more highly valued resources and assets (HVRAs).

Ignition density

Number of ignitions per unit area.

Ignition density grid

Raster-format geospatial data representing the relative number of ignitions per unit area.

Ignition frequency

Number of ignitions per unit time.

Ignition probability

The probability of an ignition occurring during the specified time period, usually one day or one year, expressed as a fraction (0-1) or a percentage (0-100).

Integrated wildfire hazard

Integrated wildfire hazard combines two important measures of wildfire—burn probability and conditional wildfire intensity—into a single characteristic that can be mapped. Integrated wildfire hazard is the product of burn probability and conditional wildfire intensity, where intensity is expressed either as the expected flame length or as the expected fireline intensity, depending upon which is used to characterize wildfire intensity.

Likelihood

Non-technical synonym for probability.

Loss

The reduction in value of a resource or asset. See net value change

Net value change

The net effect of both damaging and beneficial effects on the value of a resource or asset, whether it increases or decreases. Negative numbers for net value change indicate a net loss; positive numbers indicate a net benefit.

Pixel

A pixel—for picture element—is also called a grid cell or landscape element. It is the smallest addressable unit in a raster dataset.

Probability

The likelihood that an event will occur during a specified period of time, typically defined as the relative frequency of an event; the ratio of the number of cases that represent the event to the total number of cases.

Resource

A resource is something found in nature and necessary or useful to people—wildlife habitat, forage, timber, etc. By contrast, assets are man-made things—buildings, communication towers, roads, etc.—of value to its owner. Assets and resources can be *damaged* by wildfire, resulting in *loss* of *value*. Some resources increase in value after fire (a *benefit* of fire), but assets generally do not.

Risk

Generally, risk is the the potential for realization of adverse or beneficial consequences to HVRAs. Although there exists no single, best measure of risk, in this risk assessment framework we quantify the potential for effects as the expected value of the probability of an event occurring multiplied by the magnitude of the effect, given that and event has occurred.

Risk assessment

An appraisal of the interaction of *hazard, exposure,* and *effects* to a given set of HVRAs in a given area. Components of wildfire hazard include *the likelihood* of burning and distribution of wildfire *intensity* given that a burn occurs; both are a function of the fire environment: fuel, weather, and topography. Components of effects include intrinsic HVRA factors as well as broader environmental factors.

Risk analysis

A detailed examination including risk assessment, risk evaluation, and risk management alternatives, performed to understand the nature of unwanted, negative consequences to human life, health, property, or the environment; an analytical process to provide information regarding undesirable events; the process of quantification of the probabilities and expected consequences for identified risks.

Risk estimation

The scientific determination of the characteristics of risks, usually in as quantitative a way as possible. These include the magnitude, spatial scale, duration and intensity of adverse consequences and their associated probabilities as well as a description of the cause and effect links. (source: Society for Risk Analysis)

Risk management

"Risk Management is the identification, assessment, and prioritization of risks followed by coordinated and economical application of resources to minimize, monitor, and control the probability and/or impact of unfortunate events" (Hubbard 2009, p. 10)

Susceptibility

The propensity of an asset or resource to experience an effect as a result of burning at a given level of wildfire intensity. An asset or resource that is easily damaged by a low-intensity wildfire is susceptible, whereas one that is difficult to damage even with a high-intensity wildfire is resistant. Modifications to a building (changing to a fire-resistant roof covering, screening vents, etc.) make it less susceptible to fire damage. The term susceptibility is used for the propensity to experience either an increase or decrease in value.

Threat

The expected value of loss; nearly synonymous with risk but specifically excludes any potential for beneficial fire effects.

Uncertainty

Imperfect information or a lack of knowledge. Uncertainty can manifest in many forms, and in risk analyses often relates to understanding of the probabilities of events. Uncertainty can also relate more to knowledge gaps, linguistic confusion, or unknown preferences.

Value

The worth or importance of an asset or resource.

Value change

The change in value of a resource or asset arising from an event such as wildfire. Some resources or assets experience offsetting beneficial and adverse effects, so the term net value change is often used to acknowledge that these offsetting effects have been accounted.

Wildfire intensity

The rate of energy release of a wildfire at a point on a fire perimeter, typically measured as flame length *(FL)* or fireline intensity *(FLI)*.

Rocky Mountain Research Station

The Rocky Mountain Research Station develops scientific information and technology to improve management, protection, and use of the forests and rangelands. Research is designed to meet the needs of the National Forest managers, Federal and State agencies, public and private organizations, academic institutions, industry, and individuals. Studies accelerate solutions to problems involving ecosystems, range, forests, water, recreation, fire, resource inventory, land reclamation, community sustainability, forest engineering technology, multiple use economics, wildlife and fish habitat, and forest insects and diseases. Studies are conducted cooperatively, and applications may be found worldwide. For more information, please visit the RMRS web site at: www.fs.fed.us/rmrs.

Station Headquarters
Rocky Mountain Research Station
240 W Prospect Road
Fort Collins, CO 80526
(970) 498-1100

Research Locations

Flagstaff, Arizona	Reno, Nevada
Fort Collins, Colorado	Albuquerque, New Mexico
Boise, Idaho	Rapid City, South Dakota
Moscow, Idaho	Logan, Utah
Bozeman, Montana	Ogden, Utah
Missoula, Montana	Provo, Utah

The U.S. Department of Agriculture (USDA) prohibits discrimination against its customers, employees, and applicants for employment on the bases of race, color, national origin, age, disability, sex, gender identity, religion, reprisal, and where applicable, political beliefs, marital status, familial or parental status, sexual orientation, or all or part of an individual's income is derived from any public assistance program, or protected genetic information in employment or in any program or activity conducted or funded by the Department. (Not all prohibited bases will apply to all programs and/or employment activities.) For more information, please visit the USDA web site at: www.usda.gov and click on the Non-Discrimination Statement link at the bottom of that page.

Federal Recycling Program Printed on Recycled Paper

To learn more about RMRS publications or search our online titles:

www.fs.fed.us/rm/publications

www.treesearch.fs.fed.us

www.ingramcontent.com/pod-product-compliance
Lightning Source LLC
Chambersburg PA
CBHW080317290526
45790CB00005B/2077